A Cocktail of Clarity

How to Ditch Drinking, Embody a Joyful New
Identity and Thrive Alcohol Free

By Dupe Witherick

Terms and Conditions

LEGAL NOTICE

© Copyright 2023 **Dupe Witherick**

All rights reserved. The content contained within this book may not be reproduced, duplicated, or transmitted without direct written permission from the author or the publisher. Email requests to kevin@babystepspublishing.com

Under no circumstances will any blame or legal responsibility be held against the publisher, or author, for any damages, reparation, or monetary loss due to the information contained within this book, either directly or indirectly.

Legal Notice:

This book is copyright protected. It is only for personal use. You cannot amend, distribute, sell, use, quote, or paraphrase any part, or the content within this book, without the consent of the author or publisher.

Disclaimer Notice:

Please note the information contained within this document is for educational and entertainment purposes only. All effort has been executed to present accurate, up-to-date, reliable, complete information. No warranties of any kind are declared or implied. Readers acknowledge the author is not engaging in the rendering of legal, financial, medical, or professional advice. The content within this book has been derived from various sources. Please consult a licensed professional before attempting any techniques outlined in this book.

By reading this document, the reader agrees under no circumstances is the author responsible for any losses, direct or indirect, that are incurred as a result of the use of the information contained within this document, including, but not limited to, errors, omissions, or inaccuracies.

Published by Babysteps Publishing Limited, All enquires to kevin@babystepspublishing.com

ISBN- 9798392630479

Table of Contents

Dedication

Why I Wrote This Book	1
Why Should You Read This Book	5
My Story	9

FOUNDATION: Ditch Drinking

Chapter 1: Are You Being Served?	23
Chapter 2: The Other Side of Fear	33
Chapter 3: Design Your Life	41
Chapter 4: Only Gaining	49
Chapter 5: In The Beginning	59
Chapter 6: Open Your Mind	67

FIRSTS: Embody a New Alcohol Free Identity

Chapter 7: The First Hurdle	86
Chapter 8: It's Not About Them	108
Chapter 9: Where's The Passion	118
Chapter 10: 1440 Minutes In A Day	126

FREEDOM: Find Lasting Joy in All Areas of Life

Chapter 11: Change Your Spots For Good	138
Chapter 12: Embrace Your Emotions	146
Chapter 13: The Future Is Bright	156
Chapter 14: Dream Big	162
Closing Thoughts: (Alcohol Free) Gin Clear!	174

What Next

About The Author	178
Other Services By The Author	180
One More Thing Before You Go…	182

To my Husband, Nicholas, who has always been my greatest supporter. Thank you for all the encouragement over the years, helping me believe I can do anything I put my mind to and walking with me through this adventure called life.

To our wonderful Daughter, Iléara. I hope Generation Alpha is wiser than we were when it comes to alcohol.

Why I Wrote This Book

If you had said to me five years ago I would be alcohol free, no longer drinking and writing a book to encourage and inspire others to do the same thing, I would have initially absolutely laughed out loud, then thought (and likely said to you) that you were mad and to prove the point, would have poured another glass of fizz! At the time, there was no way I would have stopped drinking; why would I do that? I loved alcohol. It was fun, I relaxed, it gave me confidence, and I was just a normal drinker like everyone else I knew. To add to this, I was suspicious of people who didn't drink, convinced that they must lead the most boring life, and I felt sorry for them.

How wrong was I? Fast forward to today, and I've realised that by choosing to eliminate this one thing in my life, everything has changed. This is the key, a secret if you will, that not many people realise, although the younger generation is certainly becoming wise to it: by ditching the booze, you open the door to a world of opportunities, possibilities and contentment. A world where you remember your dreams and are brave enough to go after them. A world where you have a superpower!

In a society where alcohol is always there, you have a drink when you celebrate, when you commiserate, on a sunny day, on a snowy day, with your friends, with your colleagues, at home, on holiday, it's impossible to imagine life without it and the thought of deciding, **out of choice**, to not drink seems ludicrous.

Alcohol is the only drug you have to justify not taking, which seems so bizarre to me now. Many people think if you are alcohol free, there is something wrong with you, you must have hit rock bottom, or you're just boring, and they pity you! The expectation is that to have a good time, **in order to live**, alcohol is a must.

So, what if I told you that this is so far from the truth and fundamentally false? What if you are able to thrive, reach your full potential and live your best life alcohol free? Would you believe me? Probably not, so that is why I wrote this book.

This book is a guide for you if you are questioning your relationship with alcohol, wondering if life could be better without it or have started to realise alcohol is no longer serving you.

I fundamentally believe that removing this one thing from your life changes everything. It is life-changing, and many people who I've met and worked with who have gone on this alcohol free journey will agree. Anyone who is no longer drinking would never go back to it, as they have realised you are not giving up anything but, in fact, gaining so much.

I've been in the corporate world for over 20 years. I "checked all the boxes" of having a successful life but still felt like something was missing. Becoming alcohol free two and a half years ago unlocked my full potential, and I've been helping people see the benefits of quitting drinking, not as a "must" but as a choice and the positive impact it has on work, health and relationships.

My mission is to inspire as many people as I can to rethink their relationship with alcohol, choose to become alcohol free and thrive in life. We have been holding ourselves back for so long and not even realised we are doing this. By drinking, we no longer know what we really want from life, have stopped trusting our intuition and instead choose to numb ourselves through drinking. This leads to us not being fully present, not having full clarity or awareness, not appreciating nature and all that life has to offer, and the truth is you only need to be drinking a "normal" amount of alcohol to be experiencing this.

So, I hope you go on this journey with me and come out the other side realising; alcohol has been a crutch for far too long and even though we feel it makes us sophisticated and glamorous, it relaxes us and has all these benefits, we couldn't be further from the truth.

Through my THRIVE AF method, which this book is based on, you will better understand the reason alcohol has been lying to you for so long, learn how to ditch the booze, grow into your alcohol free identity and discover an exciting life that awaits you.

I hope you find this book is helpful and that it inspires you to take action, thrive, reach your full potential and live your best life alcohol free.

Why Should You Read This Book

How are you feeling today? Are you where you want to be in life? Do you feel stuck? Are you feeling anxious, stressed, or overwhelmed? Have you thought there must be more to life? Would you like to be more present with your family and friends? Do you want more clarity in life? Are you truly enjoying life?

What could thriving in life look like to you? Do you feel you are just surviving? Are you questioning whether you're drinking too much or wondering if alcohol is helping or hindering you?

The likelihood is the fact that you have opened this book; something is nudging you to explore being alcohol free. You may have become disillusioned with alcohol, started to question your relationship with alcohol, thought about whether it is still serving you, want to make a change in some way, or you are curious as to whether being alcohol free is a possibility you want to pursue. Maybe you want to discover if you are able to and if it is time to do something different, as doing the same thing month in, month out, year in year out, has given you the same results, which, although may be good, are not the results you know deep down you are capable of achieving, as you were made for so much more. So, if that is the case, this book is for you.

Although as you read this, you may be absolutely petrified at the thought of becoming alcohol free. You may be thinking, "I have always been the life and soul of the party, and everyone knows I love a glass of wine. What will people think? How will I socialise? How will I not drink on my birthday, at Christmas, or New Year? How can I go on holiday and not drink? Will I be as confident, funny, and sophisticated (fill in the blank) without alcohol? Who will I be without it?"

These questions are all valid, but they are what keep people stuck. Imagining a new alcohol free identity is hard, especially when you are doing well at work, have a good life and are quite successful, so why change? Well, because life could be even better, and you can become the person who lives a life of purpose, fulfilment, joy and peace, knowing you are living your fullest life.

Our subconscious has created so many associations over the years when it comes to alcohol. These are based on situations that have happened in our life, the habits we have formed that are associated with alcohol and how we react when we are feeling a certain way. The inevitable go-to answer is to drink. This is what keeps us stuck and, in a place, where we think alcohol is the answer, and this is what needs to change to enable us to move forward. New associations need to be created to allow us to realise that we can do other things instead of reaching for a glass of wine or a gin and tonic.

Interestingly, many of us think we can only stop drinking if we hit rock bottom and are on a park bench drinking out of a brown paper bag. However, many of us drink more than the recommended amount, and it is normal in so many facets of society that we choose not to change, not to take the first step to becoming alcohol free because why would we? Well, there are plenty of reasons why. One early hard-hitting photo that resonated with me was of a lady drinking out of a petrol can, as alcohol is ethanol. It is what we fill our cars up and clean our houses with. So, for starters, why would we want to drink that?

There is a term "Grey Area Drinkers", and this applies to everyone who is not teetotal or at rock bottom but drinks more than the recommended health guidelines.

In the UK, for men and women, this is 14 units of alcohol a week spread over three days or more, the equivalent of six medium (175ml) glasses of wine or six pints of four percent beer. Health officials in the United States recommend no more than two drinks per day for men and only one for women. While Canada is forging the way and has recently lowered their drinking guidelines to two drinks a week, and ideally, people should cut alcohol altogether! This is a substantial decrease from the 10 and 15 drinks a week for women and men, respectively, that was previously in place. However, the term "Grey Area Drinker" could also apply to anyone who feels they are drinking more than they would like to or alcohol is affecting them, even if this falls within those guidelines.

So, it is a spectrum, and the more years you have been drinking, the more likely it is you have been going down the booze elevator without even noticing, as your tolerance levels have crept up and your brain and body have learnt to cope with the amount you drink. So, if the majority of us are grey area drinkers, that means we all have a choice to go in a different direction and not be the norm.

The ultimate question to ask yourself is, "Would my life be better in all ways, if I no longer drank alcohol?" If so, you are allowed to get rid of anything that is no longer serving you, and you should read this book, as clarity is everything!

As you read this book, you will hear my story. I will pose questions for you to reflect on and encourage actions for you to take. This will help you determine whether being alcohol free is for you and will give you clarity across all aspects of your life. You will start the journey of evaluating what you want out of life, how you want to spend your time, and ultimately answer whether or not you'd like to at least try to Thrive Alcohol Free. This could mean just taking a break for a period of time, as you certainly don't need to commit to forever!

I hope this book inspires you to explore a different way of life. A life that could lead to doing things you never felt possible but always wanted to do. A life where you become the authentic person you know you are, fully living your purpose and a life in which anything is possible. I want you to know that you are brave, bold and can truly expand your capacity and thrive!

My Story

No doubt you are curious as to why I decided to become alcohol free. Before I get to that, I want to share my alcohol journey, which was obviously much longer than my alcohol free one has been, so far. However, some of the things I've achieved in a relatively short space of time makes me believe that if you have the courage to listen to your gut and ditch drinking, you will find lasting joy in all areas of your life.

I'd like to show you that I would always have classed myself as a "Normal Drinker". My drinking was not unusual, and as far as I and everyone around me was concerned, I was a high achiever, working in the City, leading projects and programmes, which involved travelling around the world. I went on fabulous vacations, hosted dinners, attended parties and just lived life. There was no rock bottom.

I thought it was important to start with this, as you may have picked up this book to try and gauge whether you actually need to make a change and question if your drinking is truly an issue for you, but the fact you're here reading this is no coincidence. I know that you want to make some sort of change in your life, you believe there is more, and you know you have been holding yourself back for some reason.

I'm hoping my story will help you see that alcohol becomes a crutch, potentially a habit that develops over time. It also becomes your identity without you fully realising or appreciating it.

You could continue drinking alcohol, and the likelihood is you will still be high achieving and highly functioning.

However, you may get to the end of your life and wish that maybe, just maybe, you should have made a change knowing you could have had a superpower that would have made you brave enough to be uncommon. I imagine, at the end of your life, you would like to know that you did not follow the crowd and actually lived the life you truly desired. You did not just sit and wait on the side-lines for the life you dreamt was possible to land on your lap, but you fully lived it.

Like most people, my drinking started around 18 years old. Before that, I'd had a few drinks when I was in sixth form, mainly cider, which I can't say I was that fond of and at home, we would have a little glass of wine every now and then, but I was always focused on studying and wanted to get good results, so didn't really drink that much until I went to university.

Freshers' week, the first week of University, is the week where the drinking culture is introduced to so many of us, and you want to fit in, so you go along to the events, do the pub crawls and drink shots, pints of beer, whatever is going. This was the start of my alcohol journey for me, and I imagine it may have been the same for you and for many others.

I was truly inaugurated into the world of alcohol, and then it just carried on. I remember in my second year, my friend and I thought, wouldn't it be fun to have at least one drink a day and record it? We thought that would be an amazing and impressive thing to do, and so the habit started. I then lived in Spain for my third year, and at the time, you could get a goldfish bowl of gin & tonic, which was really just gin topped off with tonic for 100 pesetas (50p), yes, I'm showing my age, it was before the Euro! I also discovered

red wines; Rioja and Sangre de Torro became firm favourites.

By my final year, the concept of not drinking would have been alien, it was just something I did at that time, but I believed it made me fun, gave me confidence and, most importantly, helped me to fit in, as I do remember in my first year, two girls in my University Hall didn't drink, and people just didn't speak to them, which is where my perception of people who didn't drink was boring, originally came from.

Considering everything, I did well at University and started on a Graduate Scheme in a large corporate in the City of London. I was probably not drinking as much then, but if we had team events or networking events, there was always wine involved.

As I went through my career, there were a couple of stand-out moments. In one of the organisations I worked for, there was a massive drinking culture where it was not unusual to have drinks at lunchtime, but I remember drawing the line when people were drinking Sambuca shots!

I then moved companies again, and over the next four years, I travelled for work to many countries covering all continents and was introduced to business travel and client dinners, which again seemed to revolve around drinking. I remember the first time I flew Business Class for work and was offered a glass of champagne. I felt extremely glamorous and started to associate alcohol with doing well in my career and wanted to learn about wines and do wine tasting, so I could start to speak eloquently and know what to select on the menu.

I also thought at the time I must learn to drink whiskey, even though I couldn't stand it, just to fit in with the men on my team and not feel out of place, as many of the projects I worked on were quite heavily male-dominated but I did only tend to drink when I was out, I rarely drank at home.

I don't really remember enjoying the taste of alcohol initially, but it always made me feel relaxed and in social events, it would give me the confidence to interact, and I would feel like I was an extrovert, which I'm probably not in reality, as I believe, another thing you discover as you go on this journey, is you might not be who you think you are. I feel a lot more authentic and confident now without alcohol than I ever was before.

Don't get me wrong, I had a lot of fun in my twenties and probably was the life and soul of the party and certainly known for my dancing, karaoke and having a laugh. I imagine if life had carried on like that, maybe I would have continued to be a social drinker, and it wouldn't have become the habit it did.

However, that was not meant to be. My drinking probably went up a notch in my late twenties when my brother passed away suddenly from an illness at 22 years old. This hit us so hard as a family and was such a shock, and my coping mechanism was to have a gin and tonic or a glass of red wine to numb the pain, get through and manage to put one foot in front of the other, as I tried to organise and look after everyone. It was a tough time, and that's when the drinking at home more regularly seemed to ramp up.

I imagine you may be able to relate. I've been reflecting on some of the statistics I've read about people drinking more now than pre-COVID, as well as the increase in the number of alcohol-related deaths, especially in women and wondering what has led to this. Since COVID, it seems that many people are drinking more and have developed a habit of regular "normal" drinking, even if it's only one glass a night.

Grief has been prevalent over the past few years, and many of us have grieved somehow. There has, for many, been the tragic, unexpected shock of losing loved ones, but many have also lost jobs, businesses, homes, and relationships and what they have always known has been taken from them. Nobody would have ever believed we would be told to stay at home for extended periods of time and not be able to go about our normal lives prior to this. This unprecedented situation, for many of us, has led to coping with some sort of grief. So, when we think about this, it's no wonder people have turned to alcohol, as it's helped to numb the pain and emotions and helped people to believe they are coping.

As a result, I question how many people over the past few years are realising their drinking has ramped up, and this has been due to some sort of grief. Maybe that's why you're here and reading this book. Are you walking around with a foggy head, in a bit of a daze, not fully present? Have you been able to fully process what has happened? Has alcohol become a crutch that is potentially stopping you from thriving? Although you are nowhere near rock bottom and fully functioning, you are questioning your relationship with alcohol and wondering if there is another way.

The next time I felt my relationship with alcohol change was in my Thirties, after becoming a Mum. Many Mothers will relate to this, I'm sure. The birth of my daughter was described as traumatic, and I had some health issues after the birth. Then found I did not quite feel myself for a while, and alcohol was a way to numb the feelings and adjust to a completely new way of life, which can be quite a shock to the system in the early months, especially as your body is recovering, physically and mentally and you have the huge responsibility of a little human to take care of. It's no wonder new Mums use alcohol as a bit of a crutch.

You are also suddenly being introduced to the whole Mummy wine culture and wine o'clock. It's ironic that you don't drink for nine months, which is a non-negotiable, yet as soon as you give birth, the first thing you want is a glass of champagne to celebrate and get over the birth!

Then, alcohol is promulgated as a way for Mummies to cope at the end of the day after looking after their child, as "you deserve wine"! Have you noticed the number of birthdays and Mother's Day cards that have a bottle of wine or a cocktail glass or a glass of fizz on the card? There are so few that have anything else. Then you receive emails from restaurants you're subscribed to about celebrating your birthday or Mother's Day and getting a free glass of wine or fizz. It is everywhere, and that is why as a society, it seems so normal to drink.

In our downstairs loo, we had a framed card that had a Mummy pushing a pram saying, "It's only 10:30, and I need a gin and tonic!" which I thought was quite amusing at the time, but no wonder we all feel the need to keep up and have been brainwashed to think we can't cope with life any other way! It's just seen as the norm to shove this down our throats.

Then for me, it was going back to work full time and believing that I had to prove I could do everything, and nothing had changed since I became a Mum. I was more than capable. This put unnecessary pressure on me, and a way of getting through that was to have a drink at the end of the day to unwind and relax.

Anybody, no matter how little or how much you drink, would benefit from becoming alcohol free, as your eyes are opened, and you realise how much time you have wasted and how much more you want to achieve, plus the fact you are more than capable, more than enough and can absolutely design the life you want to live.

So, that then leads to just before I ditched drinking. I never intended to still be alcohol free two and a half years in. My initial aim was to not drink alcohol for 21 days as part of giving something up for a church initiative. Stopping drinking for a certain period was something I'd tried a few times in the past, and it had always played out in the same way, so I wasn't fully convinced that 21 days would be possible.

I had tried to ditch the booze for Dry Januarys and Lents but would inevitably only do it for a week or so. The pattern was this, I'd start on a Monday, then Thursday would come, and I'd say to myself, "I've done so well, I'm sure it's ok for me to drink on the weekend…", so I would change the goal to I'll not drink during the week but can have a couple on weekends, which would inevitably end up being Friday evenings, Saturday and Sunday (who doesn't like a glass of red wine with a Sunday roast dinner!), so technically one weekday and a weekend! Then Monday would come, and the whole plan to not drink for January or Lent would have come to an end, as I wouldn't see the point. I'd already failed.

So, what was different this time? It had gotten to the point where I knew deep down that alcohol was no longer serving me. I was also aware of an internal nudge saying there was more to life and I should ditch the booze. This was coming up more often, so I was becoming more aware of it.

I used to love heavy red wine. As I mentioned, I lived in Spain for a year at 20 / 21 years old, where wine was part of the culture. I then seemed to keep this habit up when I started work and then into my 30s when I became a Mum. However, a couple of years before I stopped drinking, I found heavy red wine, like Rioja and Malbec, was no longer enjoyable, and it gave me a headache most times after just one glass. So, I switched to Pinot Noir, thinking that it was lighter, so it would be better! Then when that didn't agree, I started drinking white wine, which I had never really liked. It had always been red wine, gin & tonic and champagne that I enjoyed the most.

However, white wine was soon no longer enjoyable either; it was just gin & tonic and champagne left. I didn't mind these, but the foggy head in the mornings was becoming more of an occurrence. I didn't have a problem with alcohol. I was highly functioning, working in a pressured job in the city. I am a wife and mother and was able to hold my drink much of the time. In my head, though, I kept thinking I needed a G&T to relax and be sociable, as that was perfectly normal.

Something that I had started to notice was I needed to drink more than before to experience the same buzz that I used to get, and it was getting to the point it just felt like something I was doing out of habit and because everyone did it. However, I'd been drinking for over 20 years, so how could I possibly go to a social event, a client dinner, on holiday etc., without drinking?!

My last day of drinking alcohol was the 8th of November 2020, which was a Sunday. I knew I was going to stop for 21 days, so I thought I'd have a glass of fizz as a last hurrah! But not even halfway through that one glass, my stomach started churning, and I absolutely knew I was doing the right thing. I also had the phrase, "The truth will set you free", keep coming to me, so I thought it was time to re-evaluate. If I could stop for 21 days, that would be amazing, and then I'd be able to moderate. Little did I know this would be the start of a new, unexpected, and unimagined adventure.

I found the first couple of weeks quite tiring. I was only drinking water, coffee and tea and going to bed early. Some nights, I was in bed at 7.30 pm just to avoid thinking about drinking, as it was an ingrained habit and a way to relax in the evening. I also found I was sleeping lots, so there was no doubt my body was recalibrating.

Then everything changed, and I discovered a whole new community. I can't remember how I came across it, but I realised there were people who hadn't hit rock bottom, were "normal" drinkers and had decided to become alcohol free out of choice. I could not believe this. Why would you not drink out of choice?! However, I listened to a couple of Ted Talks on Grey Area Drinking, a term that was new to me, which basically described anyone who wasn't teetotal or had not hit rock bottom, so all drinkers! The concept was that there is a spectrum of drinkers, and my takeaway was that no matter how much you drink, if it was a problem for you, or it was no longer serving you, or you no longer enjoyed it, then you were allowed to ditch alcohol. Another one talked about how being alcohol free was great and that there were so many benefits. Both of these sparked my curiosity, and I wanted to learn more. I found out several celebrities were not / no longer drinkers, which left me dumbfounded, as being a celebrity in my mind consisted of drinking champagne and looking glamorous.

A few names you will no doubt recognise who no longer drink include Anthony Hopkins, Naomi Campbell, Bradley Cooper, Brené Brown and Denzel Washington. What was even more enlightening was that many of them said that once they stopped drinking, their careers soared, and the floodgates opened, which was encouraging.

My curiosity led me to an alcohol free podcast, which I devoured each evening, and I found an online community that inspired me to keep going. There were people in the community who were three months, six months, nine months, one year and two years+ alcohol free, and they were raving about all the benefits and how good it was. I couldn't imagine it, but I was beginning to feel differently about not drinking. I also found some alcohol free alternatives to fizz and gin that actually tasted good, which changed the game for me.

I completed an online course on ditching the booze, and the most important question was, "Why did you want to be alcohol free?". Then you were asked to consider what you liked about alcohol vs. what you didn't. As I listened to more podcast episodes, I realised most of my beliefs around alcohol and what I thought were positives, simply weren't true. I then discovered Quit Lit (books about ditching drinking), and the first one I read, where being alcohol free brought joy, completely shifted my mindset.

So, I thought I'd keep going on this journey and see what happened. Along the way, I realised I was more aware and focused. I felt I had a lot more clarity, and I was more present. I started seeing some situations for what they were and made changes. I became more patient, felt myself becoming more curious and creative and just felt an overall shift. I became more confident in my own skin, and I am convinced becoming alcohol free made me more courageous. I also found I seemed to have more time, or at least I didn't waste time, so I was reading more, learning more, doing more, not just sitting in front of the TV with a glass of wine or a G&T at the end of the day.

I got through my first alcohol free Christmas, other than when I was pregnant, by keeping the rituals, changing the ingredients and having a plan. I couldn't believe how much I enjoyed it! Normally, Christmas Eve involves wrapping presents with wine late into the night and feeling slightly heady on Christmas Morning. However, it was lovely to wake up feeling great and excited about the day this time.

I even created a vision board at the end of 2020, which I had never done. This set me up and gave me focus for 2021. I discovered self-care, which I used to think was a spa day with a glass of fizz(!) and was just looking after myself more from a well-being perspective. There were so many benefits I experienced, as I went from 21 days to 30 days, to 60 days, to 90 days, to 6 months, then a year and now two and a half years in, I can genuinely say I'm a different person and so grateful for the changes and the opportunities becoming alcohol free has brought. That is why it became a no-brainer to stay on the alcohol free path.

I am now an accredited alcohol Free Wellbeing and Transformational Coach. I work with high-achieving women who are questioning their relationship with alcohol to become the best version of themselves personally and professionally. I show them how to ditch drinking for good, embody their new alcohol free identity and find lasting joy in all areas of their life, so they can Thrive Alcohol Free! I am on a mission to help others see that alcohol could potentially be holding them back and not allowing them to reach their full potential.

Through this book, I hope to inspire you to think differently about alcohol and help you at least develop a new perspective when it comes to alcohol that will potentially transform your life, as being alcohol free changes everything!

FOUNDATION
Ditch Drinking

Chapter 1:
Are You Being Served?

"If you're asking if your drinking is problematic, then, at the very least, drinking is probably not serving you."
Brené Brown

I imagine you're probably reading this because you are questioning your relationship with alcohol. Maybe you've recently googled "Am I drinking too much?", "Am I an alcoholic?", "How do I stop drinking?" You're also probably feeling stuck in your career. Even though you're a high achiever, you know deep down there is more to life, and you are capable of so much more.

This was me. After 20-plus years of drinking, I realised alcohol had become a habit and even though I probably wasn't enjoying it as much as I previously did, it was something that I thought relaxed me, helped me fit in, and I had to keep doing it, as what would I do if I didn't drink? My view was that surely nobody would ever choose to stop drinking. You would have to have hit rock bottom or have never drunk in the first place to want to stop. Whenever I met someone who didn't drink, I was suspicious and immediately assumed they were either boring or had a problem. How wrong was I?

So, in my mind, I was convinced everyone loved drinking, and that's also what society tells us. We drink to celebrate, to commiserate, on a hot summer's day, at an event, on vacation, any excuse. It seems you need to have a drink in your hand. So, why was I the only one questioning whether alcohol was still serving me and the only one feeling this way? I was convinced everyone loved drinking, and nobody felt the way I did when I woke up at three or four in the morning feeling guilty about what I'd said or trying to remember parts of the evening/conversations I'd had the next morning.

As I mentioned in My Story, a couple of years before stopping, I realised I could no longer drink the heavy red wines that used to be my go-to, but I felt I couldn't stop drinking at that time, well actually, the truth is the thought didn't even cross my mind. My immediate reaction was to try lighter reds, which was surely the answer. However, then I went off these and thought white wine was the answer. I probably should have realised that it was alcohol that was no longer agreeing with me.

I was also getting frustrated at work. I didn't feel I was where I was supposed to be and was working with people who I thought I was just as capable as, who were in higher positions and earning much more than I was. I also started to feel more anxious, and self-doubt was creeping in, which had never really been the case. I was always quietly confident and a go getter. Little did I know alcohol is a depressant and was probably adding to my anxiety.

I would regularly find myself putting the world to rights when I was drinking after a frustrating day at work and talking about how I would change the world and the impact I could make, only to wake up the next day with a foggy head and no desire to do anything I had said the previous evening, so would go back to my day to day and continue to feel annoyed.

I was convinced there was more to life and I could do so much more, but it felt like this was a pipe dream, and I should just be grateful for where I was and not complain. My ambition was there, but I felt stuck, and in hindsight, I was undermining my capabilities and afraid to step out of my comfort zone.

I've always done exercise and probably exercised six days a week for many years, doing HIIT and Strength Training, so I was fit, but there were many times I would be doing this with a foggy head or not feeling in good form and would just push through, as I wanted to stay fit but it probably wasn't always enjoyable. I remember one time finishing a HIIT workout and doing a lower back stretch feeling a bit nauseous after over-imbibing the night before! Not a good look.

Then in 2019, the opportunity to climb Mount Kilimanjaro for a charity came up, and I thought this could be something exciting and fun and could give me something to train for and look forward to. I continued to do my regular exercise routine, but in addition, I started to walk a lot in nature in preparation for Kili. Although I was still drinking at the time, as I did these walks with my friend who was also doing the challenge, we had some great mornings and afternoons exploring areas on our doorstep that we didn't know existed, chatting and taking in the beauty around us, which I certainly had not really done for a long while.

As I was training, I realised this was the first time in many years I was doing something for myself that was really taking me out of my comfort zone. Getting all the kit and hearing about the route and what we were going to do to summit was all new and exciting, and I felt like I was doing something extremely worthwhile, especially for the charity and the children and single Mothers we were going to help.

I had a new lease of life, and I knew this experience would change me in some way. And it did. I climbed a mountain, came down, and the whole world changed! This was because I summited on the 5th of March 2020, and as you know, this was just as the world was going into lockdown due to COVID-19.

So, I had the most amazing experience. I didn't drink for six days, which was fine, but I realised I had so much time to think and had this clarity I hadn't had for a long time. Being on top of the mountain, the world felt like my oyster. I was convinced there was so much more to life, so much I wanted to achieve, and I wanted to make an impact. I didn't know how or what I wanted to do, but it changed my perspective, and I was on fire, having done something that very few people, in the grand scheme of it, had achieved and thoroughly enjoyed it! I took so many photos, learnt some word and phrases in Swahili, got to know our Guides and Porters, kept the energy high within the group and was constantly smiling (apart from one morning I found tough.) and really took everything in. It was an epic experience, so of course, once we got back to the hotel, the first thing I wanted was a glass of champagne to celebrate. How ironic and sad to me now, that after achieving something so amazing and freeing, the first thing I thought and couldn't wait for was a glass of champagne!

However, once I got back home, we found ourselves working from home a week later. The lockdown was then made official, my daughter needed to be home-schooled, and life as we knew it changed, so I didn't get a chance to explore my newfound zeal for life and think about how I truly wanted to make an impact in life, we were in survival mode, not knowing what was happening, why it was happening and how long it would last.

Work was intense, and it seemed we all wanted to justify ourselves, so I was working harder than ever. I'd be on Zoom calls from 7 am to 7 pm, we were trying to navigate this new normal, and it felt that all everyone did was work, so at the end of the day, a gin & tonic or a glass of wine was well deserved. On the Mummy WhatsApp group, the number of memes and comments around needing a drink, deserving a drink, and it being the only way to cope with children at home was unbelievable but we all bought into it. No wonder the reports now show that many people increased their drinking habits during COVID and, in some cases, to dangerous levels. It was a question of what else were we supposed to do.

So, life continued, and then towards the end of 2020, there was an initiative in my church where we were going to give something up for 21 days. It probably couldn't have come at a better time. I was questioning if alcohol was still serving me, and I had this knowing, call it the Holy Spirit, my gut, my intuition, that "the truth would set me free" if I stopped drinking for these 21 days, and this thought kept coming back to me. I didn't really know what it meant, but it was clear that I at least had to try this. Maybe alcohol was the thing that was blocking me from becoming who I was supposed to be. I mean, the definition of insanity, according to Albert Einstein, is doing the same thing over and over again and expecting different results, so something had to give. I was now in a new decade of my life, and although the previous one had been fine and there was plenty to be thankful for, I wanted this new one to be different. I wanted more. So, why not at least try?

I had no idea what to expect and had very low confidence I would stop for longer than a week, but I was determined to give it a go. Little did I know this decision would set me in a very different direction.

The first week or so was me drinking water, tea and coffee and stopping myself from drinking. What happened next could only be described as divine intervention. You could describe it as white knuckling it, knowing I just needed to get to 21 days, but it was not much fun. I went to sleep early and felt quite tired. That was my body recalibrating, and sleep really helped. It was amazing waking up feeling clear-headed.

Then I discovered Ted Talks, an alcohol free podcast and a community of people who had chosen to stop drinking and were thriving. People were enjoying what they called the "pink cloud" and raving about all the things they had done since becoming alcohol free. It was exciting to realise that there was a life outside of drinking and that you were able to enjoy life without drinking. This was completely alien to me, but I was curious about learning more.

The pièce de résistance for me was realising that there was an alcohol free "champagne" that was low calorie, low sugar and apparently the best you could get at the time. This was so mind-blowing because there was a bottle in my cupboard! Ok, let me rewind as you're probably thinking, how did she have this in her cupboard when she drinks? I mean, who has alcohol free anything, especially at that time when there were not as many options as there are now?

We had invited someone round for lunch in the summer, and he had given us a bottle of this alcohol free fizz. At the time, I thought, why on earth had he brought that, especially as he proceeded to drink wine?! Anyway, when I read about this fizz in an article, I suddenly recalled that I thought I'd seen it before and rummaged through the cupboard, and there it was, waiting for me.

This was the game changer. I had a Zoom night with the girls, and everyone was drinking fizz, so I poured myself a glass expecting it to be vile but was pleasantly surprised, and the penny dropped...if I could still feel like I was having an adult drink and not settling for tea, coffee, water or warm orange juice, enjoyed the taste and felt wonderful the next morning, why did I need to go back to alcohol.

As I also enjoyed gin & tonic, I then proceeded to look for an alcohol free gin. Again, there were not many, but one seemed to be recommended, which I tried and loved. I switched up the gin by having it with elderflower tonic, a sage leaf and a slice of orange, which again was different to my normal tipple but delicious.

I went on a Zoom call in the new community that I found, and everyone was so positive that I felt I had been missing out all this time. Imagine that! Anyway, I proceeded to ask lots of questions, as I couldn't really understand why people would choose to do this. I mean, where was the fun? Did they not feel like they were missing out? What did their friends and family think? By the end of it, I said it all sounded interesting, but I was still adamant I would only do this for 21 days because, deep down, I was scared.

Drinking had always been part of my identity. Everyone knew I liked a glass of fizz or a G&T. My husband and I drank together. We went to vineyards and tasted the wine. We had a drink with most things we did together. What would that mean if he was still drinking? The unknown was scary.

But it got towards 21 days, and I joined the Facebook group, bought my first quit lit book, and told myself I'd see if I could get to 30 days and then take it from there. The idea of stopping drinking forever seemed too far-fetched, so it was little by little in my mind.

What also helped me stay on the path was starting to learn and read about alcohol. The fact that cravings only officially last a few days and, after that, they are just thoughts, which was fascinating. Then I saw a picture of a woman drinking out of a petrol can, and this really hit home, as I had not really appreciated that alcohol is ethanol, so it is what will fill up our cars and clean our houses. Why on earth do we drink and ingest it?!

Along the way, I also learnt alcohol is the most harmful drug and biggest killer and is highly addictive. If it were introduced today, it would be banned. It is the cause of 200 illnesses, including seven types of cancer. Women who have three alcoholic drinks per week have a 15% higher risk of breast cancer. The risk increases by 10% for each additional drink a woman drinks regularly.

It impacts the brain by causing shrinkage, increases heart rate and blood pressure, negatively impacts the gut, weakens the immune system, affects sleep and can lead to type two diabetes. In addition, it can cause liver damage and liver disease. However, a positive is when you ditch drinking, it repairs itself and can regenerate, so the effects aren't lasting.

Ultimately, I felt more anxious as the years went on because alcohol is a depressant and exacerbates depression, anxiety and stress, which is the opposite of what I thought. The peak of health-related issues when it comes to alcohol is aged 45 to 55, which is pretty scary, as I'm approaching that age and who knows, if I hadn't stopped, what could have happened? All in all, the facts were not good, and we chose to drink this.

It's funny because I had always read that red wine is good for the heart or alcohol helps you sleep. Well, the research now shows that in no way is alcohol ever good for you, and in my opinion, moderation just does not work and is not worth the effort.

If you enjoy drinking and have tried to moderate, you would have found that it is near impossible and such hard work. Thoughts like: when should I drink?; I can have one today, or maybe I'll have two; It's Friday night, so I can drink, but I won't have one on Saturday all swirl around in your head. Then Saturday comes, and it's clear you want a drink, then you feel bad. All in all, it's just not fun, and all you do is think about drinking when you can be using your brain power for far more interesting and exciting activities.

The final thing that has always stuck with me is that alcohol in Arabic is AL-KUHL and means "Body Eating Spirit"! If that doesn't put you off, nothing will!!! So, when they say someone is just not themselves when they drink, this is likely why.

But I know you can read all these facts and still think, I enjoy it, I don't drink too much, so it's fine and absolutely you can stay where you are if that's what you think. There is no judgement here. All I want to show you in this book is there is a different way, which is more fulfilling, and if you are willing to keep reading, hopefully, the facts will pale into insignificance, and it will be the wonder and joy that not drinking brings that makes you want to give this whole alcohol free thing a go.

Questions to ask yourself:

1. What do you like about alcohol? What don't you like about alcohol? What do you believe it gives you?
2. Based on what you've read in this chapter, are these beliefs still true? What are your key takeaways / what resonated most on what alcohol really is?
3. How much are you drinking? On a scale of 1 to 10, with 1 being rock bottom, where are you currently when it comes to your drinking?

Action

- If you don't believe what you've read or are questioning whether what I'm saying about alcohol is true, read, research and learn what alcohol actually is for yourself.

A Cocktail of Clarity Concept

Tip: "Be open and curious about what you believe about alcohol and question it" @thrivealcoholfree

> I had so many beliefs about alcohol, and I have since learned many of these beliefs weren't true. If I hadn't been open to learning, curious and ready to challenge my beliefs, I wouldn't have seen all the benefits being alcohol free brings.
>
> So, if you are questioning your relationship with alcohol and wondering if it's still serving you, why not explore, get some information, and choose to ditch it for a period of time?

Chapter 2:
The Other Side of Fear

"What if I fail? Oh, but my darling, what if you fly."

Erin Hanson

This was the question I sometimes asked myself late at night or in the middle of the night when I woke after an evening of drinking. "Am I drinking too much?" My brain couldn't compute this, as I didn't feel I drunk that much. If I looked around and thought about how much I was drinking, I would be considered a normal drinker, and I certainly didn't have a problem. So, why did the thought of not drinking for a week seem almost impossible? Why did it seem so hard not to drink?

I realise now that it had become my identity. Everyone knew that when I was out or hosting a dinner, I would have a gin & tonic or a glass of fizz (always champagne dear, never Prosecco, as it was less sweet and, of course, so sophisticated and glamorous!), that was just who I was. I couldn't imagine life without it, even though I was enjoying alcohol less and less.

I thought it was the way to cope with everything from stress, anxiety and frustration to needing to relax, as well as something that you had to have during all occasions. I truly believed it made me more confident, I was able to be the life and soul of the party, and I had more to say when I was drinking. So, why would I stop apart from the fact I felt a little rubbish the next day?

I did start to feel that something I once thought was fun was now no longer serving me, and I realise now that even though I didn't think I was anxious at the time, as I went through my first 21 days, I realised that I was anxious to some degree, especially when it came to work. I also found I was second-guessing myself, thinking about what I'd said or didn't and not really remembering much. And, of course, at the time, I didn't realise that alcohol was exacerbating my anxiety.

In hindsight, I probably wanted to stop drinking or maybe drink occasionally, but I was afraid. My fear of stopping drinking was twofold. Firstly, I wondered if I could actually stop. Everyone I knew drank, and that was what I was known for, so why would I need to stop unless I had a problem, and what would others think if I did stop? Secondly, if I didn't drink, what did that mean? What would life be like on the other side?

I don't think at the time, I ever thought I would not drink again, but I knew I wanted to be able to feel like I could go weeks without booze and not miss it or feel the fear of missing out. I no longer wanted to wake up feeling rubbish with a thick, foggy head most mornings, dreading the day. I wanted to be more present and able to spend quality time with my daughter and not feel like it was an effort. I wanted to live the life I knew I was supposed to live and be the best version of myself.

I wanted to remember things that had happened, as my memory seemed to be going, especially my short-term memory. I didn't want to wake up thinking about what I did or said or who I offended. Overall, I wanted to be a better

Wife and Mum and to feel calmer internally, patient and in control. Many people thought I was a calm person, as I didn't get flustered in situations and could calm others, but internally, I felt anxious.

However, there were many reasons why I didn't want to stop drinking. I was nervous about social situations. I knew it would make me different, and I wasn't sure what impact that would have on existing relationships and friendships. My husband and I had been together for 20 years, and a lot of what we did together would involve a drink, so I was mindful that if I didn't drink even for 21 days, would I be able to do it, and how would it impact us?

The other thing that played on my mind was other people. This is really common. As women, we worry about what other people think, or many of us are people pleasers. I thought people would think I had a problem with alcohol, and I also thought that I wanted to fit in, so the people pleaser in me didn't want to offend others by not drinking, which is probably what got me to that point in the first place!

I didn't know how I would manage work situations such as client dinners, conferences etc., as this always revolved around drinking wine.

I also thought I enjoyed the taste of alcohol, which used to be a treat, but then it became a habit, a go-to after a day at work, a way to relax and let go of the day, and it also felt like a reward. So, as well as a fear of missing out, there was also the fear of missing alcohol.

As I progressed through this journey, though, I started to challenge some of these thoughts. Were they true? I also realised I spent a lot of time thinking about drinking, and it took up so much headspace, way more than I could ever have imagined. When I thought about how I felt after the first drink, I would say I was calmer, relaxed, able to conquer the world and less nervous in a social situation, could hold my own in a conversation and was able to speak my mind more easily. I also felt people gravitate towards me when I was drinking.

But when I thought about how I felt after the third or fourth drink, that was a different story. I either felt a bit hazy and couldn't remember certain conversations, or I was the life and soul of the party depending on how much I'd drunk or how strong the drinks were. If they were strong drinks, I felt pissed and was probably thinking about why I had so much and dreading how I'd feel the next day.

The picture I'm trying to paint here is that I didn't think I had a problem with alcohol, but it had become a habit. I was no longer enjoying it but I was still drinking, in order to people please and fit in. I continued drinking and found it tough to stop or imagine life without it.

On the other side, I am now aware that alcohol has that effect, and the longer you drink, the more you will struggle to do without it because alcohol is an addictive substance. Although you may think that alcohol isn't addictive and at the moment you're fine, the fact is it takes a long time to get addicted to it, and your brain has made so many associations over the years with alcohol that it becomes an automatic response. We are ultimately using alcohol to escape from feelings or create specific feelings and need to retrain the brain to find other coping mechanisms or ways to manage those feelings without alcohol.

Towards the end of the 21 days, I came to the understanding that my life could be better physically and emotionally without it, so I had to give myself permission to change, to not drink for a bit longer and see where it led to. I concluded that I should at least try, even if I did end up drinking again and feel I've failed, as what did I have to lose?

If you are reading this, maybe you need to hear this. You are allowed to change. You can choose to have a different identity. You are allowed to be who you are and permit yourself to be who you are meant to be, as you are unique and are here for such a time as this, for a reason, and you can do something different. Maybe everything you believe about alcohol and who you are now simply isn't true, and you can decide to question this.

It is easy to stay in your comfort zone because you fear change or do not want to do something that others may judge you for, as you fear rejection, but it is so worth it, and you are worth it.

Being alcohol free is an ever-growing trend, and an alcohol free community is cheering you on, as we are on the other side and know what a difference being alcohol free is. It is the best-kept secret, and it gives you wings to go out and do whatever you may have dreamed of in the past and have real confidence to go after it. There is even a wonderful hashtag, #weretheluckiest, which I believe is the case.

Are you ready to give yourself permission and have faith instead of fear? I believe you're reading this for a reason, and the best is yet to come, so I do hope the answer is a resounding yes!

I wrote down my "Why" for becoming alcohol free in my tracker, where I could track days and money saved.

My why in all its unfiltered glory: *"I don't want to feel foggy every morning and feel like I struggle to engage and make the most of my day. I want to be more present for my Daughter and Husband and remember what they tell me and everything about my life. I want to have more energy and clarity and live my best life by being the best version of myself. I want to not do stupid things I later regret when I'm drunk, and I want to stay calm and be less anxious at work."*

This is unfiltered, and when I read it again, it does sound like I must have had an issue, however, I know, I was fully functioning, doing regular exercise, going on fabulous holidays, leading big teams and projects and travelling the world for work. I even climbed Kilimanjaro! So, you could conclude it wasn't an issue. However, the crux of it is no matter how much you drink, only you can answer if alcohol is really serving you and whether life could be better without it. Nobody else. For me, it was time to let go, at least for a little while, as something had to change, and I didn't want to waste any more time.

Questions to ask yourself:

1. Why do you want to be alcohol free? Why don't you want to be alcohol free?
2. What's stopping you from becoming alcohol free?
3. When you drink, what feelings are you trying to escape from, or what feelings are you looking to create?

Action

- Write at least ten sentences on why you want to stop drinking.

A Cocktail of Clarity Concept

Thought: "If fear is stopping you from becoming alcohol free, take a step in faith today, and you will find something amazing on the other side of fear." @thrivealcoholfree

> Do you know deep down that your life could be better without alcohol but worry that people may think you have a problem with booze, you won't be fun anymore, or you're not convinced it is possible to do life without alcohol?
>
> Can I encourage you to at least take one step today to overcome whatever the fear is and have faith that even though you may not know what will happen, just by taking a step forward, you are allowing yourself to explore a new possibility?
>
> You do not need to have reached rock bottom to stop. You can absolutely change even though you are a "normal" drinker if that is something you'd like to do.
>
> Go on, have faith over fear and take that first step today.

Chapter 3:
Design Your Life

"Recognising that you are not where you want to be is the starting point to begin changing your life."

Deborah Day

As I was going through the start of my alcohol free journey, I started to think about what life would be like without it longer term. When I initially stopped drinking for 21 days, I was not convinced there would be a reason for me to stop for longer than that. All I wanted to do was prove to myself that I could do a long stint without drinking.

2020 for all of us had been a very unexpected year. COVID-19 had literally stopped the world and questioned everything we thought was true about life. We were told we could only leave the house for exercise for one hour a day. We couldn't socialise. Going to buy food was a massive challenge. I remember queuing for hours to get into our local supermarket, and when you got in, the shelves were not stocked, and toilet roll, especially, was impossible to get hold of! Shops, restaurants, and hairdressers were all closed.

For those of us who had children, they were not at school, and we, as parents, were tasked with home-schooling and keeping them entertained while juggling work in some cases. The normal we had been so used to was suddenly taken away, and we were navigating a new norm.

So, the easiest thing to do at the end of the day to reduce stress and feel like you were in control of the situation was to have a drink. The number of WhatsApp messages I received from the School Mums group and friendship groups were all about needing to drink to survive effectively.

The start of 2020 had been exciting. It was a new decade. I was climbing Mount Kilimanjaro in March, turning 40 in April, and I had big plans to celebrate in style. Going into the year, there were murmurings of something in Wuhan, China, but we never suspected how the year and the subsequent years would turn out.

I summited Mount Kilimanjaro on the 5th of March, which was a massive achievement. The experience was epic. Over 30 of us were climbing for charity, and we had porters and guides, so 100 of us went up and down the mountain over six days camping out. An experience like that is bound to change you, and for me, I wanted to make the most of it and be present.

I took so many photos to capture the experience. I enjoyed taking in the scenery and landscape. I loved going from really hot to snow blizzards and then back through the hot jungle on descent seeing various monkeys, butterflies and wildflowers. I learnt some Swahili, and I laughed, sang and cried. I was fine the whole week, taking it all in my stride, eating everything and making new friends, but one morning, mid-week, I felt quite emotional and seemed to wake up like that. Then I spilt water all over my bag, had to rush breakfast, and it all felt too much. As an aside, I wonder now if that was a few days of not drinking and my body was beginning to recalibrate, but not knowing what I know now, this wasn't even a thought. However, I felt much better when we walked to the next campsite, listened to music, and enjoyed the vast expanse that looked like a dessert seeing the odd crow.

Not everyone managed to summit. Some people got ill, others struggled with the altitude and breathing, and some just physically weren't able to make it, so I was enormously grateful to have had the experience and had managed to get through it in a way that was positive and so life-giving.

I remember having a couple of drinks the night before we went to start the climb but then didn't drink for six days while we went up and down and didn't really miss it, but as soon as I got back to the hotel after such an amazing feat, the first thing I wanted to do was celebrate with a glass of champagne! Looking back, I'm really not sure why, as I was certainly on a natural high and was thinking about what I could do to make the most of life and do more and be more, which in hindsight, probably led me to ditch alcohol for good.

So, I climbed a mountain, came down, and the world changed! I arrived home and was so excited to tell everyone what I'd achieved, share photos and discuss the experience, but all anyone was talking about was COVID. At the time, we had an au pair, and she was saying she might have to return to Germany. I went for a celebratory drink with a friend at our local gastro pub, which was normally busy, but I think we were the only ones there. Chatting to the Manager, he said that people had stopped coming in. It was surreal.

Before I left, Italy had it and was locking people down, but within less than two weeks, there was a sense that this wasn't going to be a normal experience, but we didn't know the extent. My daughter's birthday was the day before I landed, so we'd bought tickets to see The Lion King in the West End the following Saturday. I remember seeing a family with masks on, which they wore throughout the show, and I thought, what's that about, weren't they being way over precautious? Little did I know all the theatres would be shut the following Wednesday?

On the Monday, I went into the office, and they said we would all try working from home the next day, and that was it. I didn't go back to that office ever! So, we were in lockdown, believing it would only be a couple of weeks, and drinking was a coping mechanism. My birthday came, and I was sent so many bottles of champagne (and flowers). It was unbelievable, but I couldn't celebrate in style as I'd planned, but I did drink lots of champagne. At the end of the day, though, I thought I really didn't need to and just felt sleepy. On reflection, drinking champagne on my birthday was a tradition for many years. I remember when I was pregnant with our daughter, the only time I didn't drink for nine months, that as soon as I gave birth, I couldn't wait to drink again. My birthday fell before I was pregnant and just after I was pregnant, and drinking champagne was a must, so probably since I was a teenager, I hadn't gone without a glass of champagne on my birthday!

Anyway, during COVID, the habit of drinking was more of a daily occurrence, and it was clear, like so many, that it was just something to do. Research has since come out that suggests many people were drinking more than they would have previously.

A combination of the exhilaration of climbing Kilimanjaro, seeing a new decade plus some disappointments at work and knowing there was more to life and that I could achieve so much more led me to think about my drinking. As the year progressed, I started getting these little nudges that maybe I'd be better off not drinking for a little bit, and this started to get stronger, but I didn't think I could change my life, design and be intentional in the life I wanted to create.

Having taken a step of faith, I started to think about my life, mostly my work role and as I went through the month, I got some unexpected and disappointing news about work and realised I was no longer in the right place. I was not being valued, and it was time to seriously consider what to do next. If I had been drinking, I would have repeated what I'd always done in the past. I would have got annoyed, turned to booze, gone on about how I was so much better than what I was currently doing, I wasn't appreciated, and I'd show them but would have proceeded to stay stuck, as I would wake up the next day, have been too anxious to change the status quo, questioning whether I was good enough to do something else and carried on sucking it up.

Having not been drinking, I realised I was worth so much more, could change the situation, and had the network, ability and expertise to do something different. For the first time in many years, I was backing myself and open to having conversations with people from other companies about opportunities and seeing where they led.

I was also beginning to feel I wanted to make more of an impact on people and asked myself if I could do something completely different. I've always enjoyed the coaching courses I'd done at work over the years and love helping people see their inner potential and encouraging them to see their gifts, so I also thought about a complete change of career. At the time, though, the main thing for me was I was allowing myself to think clearly and make choices. I had less anxiety and was beginning to believe again that the world was my oyster, having got so caught up since COVID had started.

I was questioning what I wanted to do in life and whether remaining alcohol free for a longer period of time could help towards this. My thoughts were changing about things in general. I no longer wanted to work all hours. I wanted balance, as there didn't seem to be much balance. I started to think about values and designing a life that would incorporate all elements, so I was more rounded and could intentionally enjoy life more.

My thoughts were changing, which was impacting how I felt and making me take action!

Questions to ask yourself:

1. What is working in your life, and what isn't?
2. What do you anticipate being alcohol free could look and feel like?
3. How long do you want to stop drinking for, and what will most likely get in the way of this goal?

Action:

- Write down what you'd like life to be like without alcohol.

A Cocktail of Clarity Concept

Tip: "If you're thinking you were meant for more or that there's more to life, consider whether ditching alcohol could help." @thrivealcoholfree

We are capable of so much, and we have endless potential. However, we hold ourselves back from doing what we really want or living our fullest life.

If you know, you are meant for more but feel stuck. Maybe alcohol is getting in the way, and taking a break could just be what you need to take a different path.

What is your soul telling you? What do you know deep down?

Listen to it and see where it takes you.

Chapter 4:
Only Gaining

"When I got sober, I thought giving up (alcohol) was saying goodbye to all the fun and all the sparkle, and it turned out to be just the opposite. That's when the sparkle started for me."

Mary Karr

I imagine you may be thinking, "ok, so I know alcohol isn't serving me, and maybe I should take a break. I also can get over the fear of not stopping and what others think, and I do have thoughts on how my life could be better, or I'm excited that I can potentially design the life I want."

However, in your mind, you still believe you are giving alcohol up and feel like you will be deprived in some way if you ditch drinking. Can I stop you there? When you think about ditching drinking, I'd like you to know you are not giving anything up. You are only gaining, and what I mean by gaining is there is absolutely nothing you will miss out on or regret if you take this first step. You also don't need to look at this as ditching drinking forever, as that will be a lot for your mind to process, so don't put so much pressure on yourself.

Alcohol is so ingrained in our lives and society that it feels like you have to give something up and you'll be missing out, but what if that is not the case? What if by becoming alcohol free and not following the crowd, you actually find you're gaining and enjoying the benefits and opportunities it brings? What if instead of the fear of missing out, you experience the joy of missing out? What if being alcohol free leads to you living your best life and being the best version of yourself? Is it worth trying to at least see if you could experience a little bit of that and the difference it could make in your life?

All you have to think for now is: "I know that I have a nudge telling me that maybe not drinking for a bit will be beneficial in some way. I'm unsure what will transpire, but I'm willing to be open and curious and start on the right foot. I will look at what I will gain from ditching drinking, observe what happens during the time I commit to, and be open to see what transpires."

One of the things I encourage clients to do is celebrate milestones and make a note of the benefits they are seeing along the way, as you then start to create new neuropathways in your brain that allow you to change what you have learnt over the years when it comes to alcohol and create new habits. I find people have more clarity and awareness, grow, move more and are happy with themselves when they look in the mirror, which may be for the first time in a long time.

The benefits you get from becoming alcohol free over time are so amazing, and the opportunities and experiences that come to you make you realise you have not given up anything. You are only gaining. There is no need to white knuckle it through or take it one day at a time because your mind will be blown by the endless possibilities and doors that open, and you are brave enough to take them on, go after them and win!

The first month can be tricky, but even in that first month, you will see that you're waking up with more energy, you're feeling clearer, anxiety is reducing, and potentially your sleep is getting better. But as time goes on, it gets better and better.

Some of the benefits I saw early on included being more present, taking more in, enjoying spending time with my daughter, having better focus, awareness and mental clarity, experiencing less anxiety, trying new things, being open and curious and feeling generally healthier.

When I was in my early days, I kept hearing about people who had experienced pink clouds, and I was curious about what that meant. Pink clouds is a term that is used in the alcohol free world when you get to a point, maybe three to six months in and experience a euphoria like never before. And all the work of getting to that point is worth it as you realise how incredible life is and could be. It feels like the scales have come off, and you know a secret that many will never choose to experience.

Not everyone goes through this, but it doesn't matter because you soon experience the many benefits of not drinking, and you realise you are not giving up anything, only gaining.

To inspire you and emphasise that you are not giving anything up when you ditch drinking but only gaining, I'd like to give you 25 reasons to ditch the booze for 100 days or more.

1) You really **start to see the full benefits** of not drinking. After 30 days, you feel slightly better but won't appreciate the power of being alcohol free. Also, you may be just waiting for the 30 days to end

and thinking about when you can have your next drink if you only do 30 days!
2) You will likely have found some **amazing new hobbies** by 100 days that will likely be much more satisfying than drinking and give you a different perspective on what is fun!
3) You will have **clarity** in all aspects of your life, which will help you evaluate what you really want out of life and how you want to spend your time.
4) Any **anxiety will have pretty much disappeared**. We think it is normal to be anxious, but alcohol exacerbates anxiety, and it is amazing how when you ditch the booze for 100 days+, that anxiety is so much less.
5) You will find a **new alcohol free community**. People around you may not understand why you're ditching the booze, especially as it's so normalised in our society, but there's a community of like-minded people waiting to embrace you!
6) You will have more **energy and excitement** about life and realise how much **time** there is and that you don't want to waste it!
7) You will **be more aware** of what is and isn't working in your life and be able to decide what is next.
8) You will be **more present** in life and learn to live in the moment. This will impact how you interact with your nearest and dearest.
9) You will become **brave**! Being alcohol free helps you realise who you really are and allow yourself to do and try things you wouldn't have dared to do before.
10) You will have more **drive and ambition**, leading to discovering your **purpose**.

11) You will have found **joy in the little things**, such as walking in nature, and you will notice so many more things around you.
12) You will have discovered an **alcohol free toolkit** that works for you, which will help you sustain your alcohol free identity.
13) You will start to **change the trajectory** of your life and your family's life.
14) You will have **brighter eyes** and **clearer, less puffy skin**.
15) You will truly see the difference in your sleep quality and start to **dream again**!
16) You will likely have gone through several alcohol free firsts, meaning you will feel **stronger in your alcohol free identity**.
17) You will feel **healthier** and likely to be **eating better** and taking up some form of **exercises** such as running, yoga or cold water swimming!
18) You will have developed new **morning** and **evening routines** that help you start and end your day correctly.
19) You will realise you are **creative** and become more **curious**, enabling you to live the life you want.
20) Lots of **positive things** will start to happen, and you will find **new opportunities** coming your way.
21) You will have learnt and actually taken in the fact that **alcohol is ethanol**, which is what fuels our cars, and it causes 200 illnesses and seven types of cancer. So why do we think it's the best thing ever and we need it in every situation? I am not sure.
22) You will feel **calmer** and have developed better coping skills.
23) You will feel **free** and **content** and be your **authentic self**.

24) You will realise ditching drinking is not weird, and there is an **amazing life** to be had without booze!
25) You will feel **so proud**, as this is a massive achievement!

I have spoken to people who have convinced themselves they are not going to benefit at all by not drinking, nothing will change, and when they imagine themselves in a year's time, they believe they will have achieved the same things regardless of whether they have ditched drinking or not. However, in the same breath, they say, "But alcohol is the one thing I can't control even though, I am healthy, I exercise 5 to 6 times a week, I eat well, I have a great family life, I can still get the promotion, but I suppose I could be more present with my children."

This, to me, is a red flag, as if you are so disciplined and can do all the things, why are we even having the conversation? The reality is alcohol is an addictive substance, and you become more dependent over time, and that's why people think they can't control it. Even though you don't want to give up your girls' night with a couple of drinks or your Friday night of curry and a glass of wine with your husband, or pizza with your children with a glass of fizz on a Saturday night, it is worth considering if life would be better without it. One thing we do know is it's generally not just one or two glasses. The likelihood is alcohol has become so ingrained, and your perception of what is a great life, which no doubt it is, is potentially watered down or numbed to what could potentially be an amazing life.

My life was great. I did all the things. I had a good job. I travelled the globe for work. We went on lovely holidays. We socialised with friends. We hosted fab dinner parties. I exercised six days a week, encouraged people and enjoyed time with my Husband, daughter and dog. But this is the big thing. Something was not sitting well with me. I felt I was holding myself back. I wasn't reaching my full potential. I could do so much more. I could make more of an impact. But in the same breath, I didn't think alcohol was that big a deal, and surely ditching this one thing wouldn't make that much of a difference.

Yet, I couldn't have been more wrong. As I said in month one, I started to see benefits, but I wanted to share my top three benefits that I experienced every six months and the impact these had on my life, since I ditched drinking. This is not to brag but hopefully inspire.

6 Months Alcohol Free

- I'd got through a few alcohol free firsts, Christmas, New Year, Birthday, which helped me grow in confidence when it came to being alcohol free.
- I'd started a Transformational Coaching qualification, which ended up also being a personal growth journey for me.
- I'd run my first 10k, having not run since school. When I started the 10k program, I remember feeling so pleased with myself that I was able to run for fifteen minutes without stopping!

12 Months Alcohol Free

- I'd started a new job, which was my dream job and significantly increased my earning power.
- I'd qualified as an accredited Transformational Coach and coached a number of people, helping them with various life challenges, which I found incredibly fulfilling.

- I'd read more books in a year than I had done in the past ten years and completed a number of personal development courses, which opened my eyes to so many things.

18 Months Alcohol Free

- I ran my first half marathon, did my first abroad alcohol free vacation, which I absolutely loved and qualified as an Alcohol Free Wellbeing Coach, all of which helped me learn something about myself and grow as a person.
- I was diagnosed with a rare illness but was able to cope well due to the tools and habits I'd developed since being alcohol free.
- I founded Thrive Alcohol Free, which came to me so clearly, along with my signature method, and I believe this was due to my spiritual growth.

24 Months Alcohol Free

- I recovered well from my illness, which I was told could have been chronic and did not need ongoing treatment.
- I had two abroad business trips where being alcohol free didn't bother me.
- I ran my second half marathon, which I did not think would have been possible a few months earlier, due my health issues!

30 Months Alcohol Free

- My Husband ditched drinking, which was an unexpected miracle!

- I trained for five days a week for 18 weeks and ran a marathon, plus I've practised yoga pretty much every evening since being two months alcohol free
- I created and launched Thrive Alcohol Free Society and wrote a book that was published!

What benefits could you see if you were to stop drinking? Could you be less anxious, more present, healthier, go out and find your ideal job, be more financially free, have more quality time to spend with family and friends, grow your faith, pick up a new passion, or have more clarity? What would help you see you're only gaining and not giving up anything? I'm excited for you, as you're on the cusp of something amazing once alcohol is no longer a thing.

Questions to ask yourself:

1. Which benefits of becoming alcohol free are you most excited about?
2. What are your desires and dreams for your life if you become alcohol free?
3. If you didn't ditch drinking, do you believe you could still achieve these dreams and desires?

Action:

- Write down five things you'd like to achieve from being alcohol free.

A Cocktail of Clarity Concept

Tip: "Focus on what you're gaining, as you are not giving anything up!" @thrivealcoholfree

> When I ditched drinking, I gained clarity and awareness, and opportunities came unexpectedly. This helped me start to see I wasn't giving up

anything, only gaining and experiencing life completely differently.

Chapter 5:
In The Beginning

"You can. You should. And if you're brave enough to start, you will."

Stephen King

You've been reading for a few chapters now, and maybe you think I want to try this, so where do I start, and how do I stay on the path for however long I choose to be alcohol free? Well, I will give you some practical steps that will get you started and hopefully make you want to continue on the journey.

As you have written your why and know the reason(s) you want to stop, keep this somewhere close where you can reference it, especially when you've had a tough day at work and life happens, so you are not tempted to reach for a glass at least for the period you agree to stop drinking for.

I suggest you try to do at least 100 days alcohol free and make it non-negotiable. You may think this seems too long, but it is the optimal time to allow your body to recalibrate, build new skills, experience alcohol free firsts, start to embody and become comfortable in your alcohol free identity and really see the benefits. Of course, it's totally up to you what you commit to, so you could say you'll do 60, 30 or 21 days (like me), but whatever you commit to, why not start today? Make a decision and go for it!

Then tell someone. Feel free to contact me and let me know you are doing this, as it will help you feel accountable and means you don't have to tell everybody. The likelihood is if you tell someone who has not been through it, they will not understand and probably say, but you don't have a problem, and surely you can have one, and before you know it, you start to second guess yourself and wonder if it's worth it. This is your decision, you only have one life, and you don't want others to influence you negatively, so you give up before you start.

Then download a tracking app where you can see the days, how much money and time you're saving and celebrate every milestone, so you can appreciate what you are achieving. This journey may not be easy at the start, but it's so worth it, and by noting the milestones, you can be proud of how far you've come and hear others' stories as well.

In the beginning, you should focus on nutrition and sleep. You will find you are more tired, as your body recalibrates, but you also need to nourish your body with good food. This is not the time to diet. You need to focus on this one thing. The rest will come.

You need proper healing food with healthy fats, such as avocados, nuts, seeds and oily fish. You should not have anything low fat, low sugar, artificial sweeteners or anything with aspartame. This is not just for now, but overall, anything low fat/sugar with aspartame is not real food. Aspartame is also a waste product, so never a good thing to ingest! So, make sure you eat three meals a day and have protein every meal.

When you stop drinking, you realise how much sugar alcohol contains, as you find you'll crave sugar a lot more. I get asked about this all the time, and yes, it is perfectly normal. Alcohol contains a lot of sugar, so when you ditch it, your body wants to replenish it, so try stevia or coconut sugar as alternatives. If you experience sugar cravings and this is something that is worrying you, try some healthy alternatives, such as dark chocolate energy balls or Medjool dates, as these can help. Juicing is also great and helps you eat good portions of fruit and vegetables every day. Green juice always takes any cravings away. Below are two recipes to make to help with sugar cravings.

Dark Chocolate Energy Balls Recipe

- 45g old-fashioned rolled oats
- 37g ground flaxseed
- 1.5 tablespoons regular unsalted cocoa powder
- 0.5 tablespoon brown sugar
- One tablespoon of chia seeds
- 40g dark chocolate chips
- One tablespoon of coconut oil melted
- 43g honey
- 40g smooth peanut butter

Mix all these together in a large bowl, put this in the fridge for 10 minutes, then create balls by rolling them into one-inch balls and eat! You can keep them in the fridge, and you can have them anytime you have a sugar craving. Enjoy!

Green Juice: Many recipes are out there, so feel free to look up alternatives. However, the below is one where I originally experimented with the ingredients, and I love:

- Two green apples
- One whole lemon
- Three celery sticks

- A couple of chunks of ginger (so good for the immune system)
- A couple of handfuls of spinach
- Broccoli stem
- One teaspoon of spirulina (optional)
- One teaspoon of wheatgrass (optional)

I found with sleep it took me a while to get into a good sleep pattern. As I've mentioned, I slept a lot the first couple of weeks, but I remember struggling to sleep as well, and that seemed to go on for months, but I was always waking up better regardless of how much or little sleep I had.

Alcohol affects REM sleep, as it is a sedative, which is a cycle of sleep where your brain is almost as if you are fully awake. This is also the sleep where you dream, so when you ditch the booze, and your REM sleep goes back to the normal cycles, you literally start to dream again! Even if you only have one glass of wine, your REM sleep is still affected, which is why you feel groggy or foggy headed, as you are not getting enough REM sleep. You should go through six to seven cycles of REM sleep every night, but drinkers generally only get two.

Things like not drinking coffee after 2 pm, eating at least three hours before bed, minimising screen time and establishing an evening routine can all help with sleep. I will go into more detail on building habits and daily routines in Chapter 10.

Then, I'd suggest learning as much as possible through reading Quit Lit, listening to Podcasts, following alcohol free influencers on Instagram, joining alcohol free Facebook Groups, potentially participating in one-to-one or group coaching for additional support guidance and finding a community.

By reading my first quit lit book, my eyes were opened, and I realised that not drinking was actually a really positive thing and a pure joy! This was amazing!!! As you are reading this book, you've already started on the Quit Lit journey, but it is so interesting reading other people's stories and learning from others, as it allows you to reflect on your own journey, and something always resonates.

With everyone busy on the go, there is the audible option or podcasts, which are so handy if you have a 30-40 min drive or doing something and can't sit and read. So many alcohol free podcasts have popped up over the past few years, which makes it really accessible, and I find them inspiring and motivating. Listen to a few and find your favourites.

Then one of my favourite suggestions for trying in the early days are alcohol free drinks. Our inner toddler doesn't want to feel like it's missing out, which triggers cravings, and later thoughts and causes people to reach for a drink if they don't feel they have an adult drink, so alcohol free drinks, in a way, trick the mind. Some people prefer not to go down this route, but for me, it was one of the reasons I stayed on the path.

There are so many options now, and there is so much variety compared to even a couple of years ago, so why not investigate what is available and try a few different ones? You should be able to find an alcohol free substitute for your favourite tipple. Make sure you have it in an adult glass and discover what works. People ask about the percentage levels, as there are drinks that are 0.5%. Anything up to 0.5% is considered alcohol free, as this is the same percentage of alcohol that is in a ripe banana, so you are good to go with anything 0.5% ABV (alcohol by volume) or below.

In terms of supplements, eating proper food three times a day should be fine. However, Magnesium is a good supplement to take, especially in the early days, as it regulates mood, sleep and anxiety. You could also consider vitamin D and vitamin C.

You want to spend the first 30 days feeling as well as you can, and then you can go from there.

I continued to exercise, as normal, when I stopped drinking because I'd always done that, but also found going for walks in nature helped. Do not worry about losing weight, and don't deprive yourself of anything, as that is not the purpose of ditching drinking.

Good nutrition will help with so many things, so maybe invest in a juicer and think about what you're eating. As mentioned earlier, have three meals a day and protein with each meal. Also, avoid anything low fat or low sugar. Anything with Aspartame is not good, so check for this. Finally, make sure you take in really good fats such as olive oil, sunflower oil, avocados, and nuts. Plus, having healthy snacks available when you feel you'd like something, so you don't automatically reach for something sugary!

Finally, remember, cravings are just thoughts, and people often have cravings not because they actually want a drink but because they are hungry. So, if you have a craving while you are making dinner, the likelihood is you may be hungry, so eat!

Questions to ask yourself:

1. What is inspiring you to be alcohol free for a period of time?
2. What resources do you already have to help you on your journey?
3. How would you like to feel?

Action:

- Find a quit lit to read, a podcast to listen to or an alcohol free drink you think you will enjoy and read a few chapters, listen to at least one episode or try the drink.

A Cocktail of Clarity Concept

Tip: "Get sleep & good nutrition in the early days" @thrivealcoholfree

> You may find sleep is varied. I remember the first couple of weeks taking myself off to bed to read and get an early night, so I could break my normal pattern, which may have tempted me to "just have one", but I also felt quite tired.

> I suggest sleeping when you need to, but you may find sleep tricky at the beginning. I struggled with sleep a couple of months in and thought I'd never sleep properly again, as this seemed to last forever, but it was probably only a month or two. However, everyone's different. Now, on the whole, I sleep really well and feel fully rested when I wake up ready to start the day, so it does get better and waking up without a foggy head never gets old.

Nutrition is also key in the early days, and ensuring you eat well is essential. Please be mindful that this is certainly not the time to diet. You can look at that at a later date, if necessary.

Chapter 6:
Open Your Mind

"You can rise up from anything. You can completely recreate yourself. Nothing is permanent. You are not stuck. You have choices. You can think new thoughts. You can learn something new. You can create new habits. All that matters is that you decide today and never look back."

Idil Ahmed

You've worked through the why and have discovered how to get started, but no doubt you're asking what the practical steps are. How can I really get started on this alcohol free journey or ditch drinking for a period of time and not feel like it's a chore or that I can't get past the cravings?

This chapter will review the tools and resources you need and some practical steps to help you succeed.

First and foremost, it is worth creating an alcohol free toolkit. This will help you have go-to tools and resources that will be an alternative to drinking or stop you from automatically reaching for a drink.

There are eight things that I suggest you include in your alcohol free toolkit, and then you can pick and choose what is helpful to you at any given point.

1) **Quit Lit & Podcasts**

   One of the main reasons I initially stuck with not drinking in the first couple of weeks was discovering the truth about alcohol and realising there was a whole community of people out there who didn't drink out of choice and were thoroughly enjoying life!

   It sounds ridiculous now, especially as the alcohol free movement has grown so much over the past few years. However, I always thought people who didn't drink were boring, and I would be the one convincing them they needed to have a drink and not understanding why you wouldn't want at least one. Why on earth wouldn't you want a drink?

   Anyway, I stumbled across a couple of Ted Talks that resonated. I then went on to listen to an amazing alcohol free podcast, which I binge-listened to in the first weeks and months, and it definitely helped give me a completely different perspective.

   Finally, I heard about and read my first Quit Lit (books about ditching drinking), and my mindset started to shift. I realised that by ditching the booze. I wasn't losing anything, but I potentially could gain a lot!

   Hopefully, if this book is your first introduction to Quit Lit, this is inspiring you, but please explore the others. There are so many wonderful authors out there who have incredible stories that will no doubt keep you encouraged and get you to appreciate, at least in the first few months, that although they all have been on different journeys, they have all inevitably discovered the best kept secret, that being alcohol free is the greatest gift and only helps you to live the life you want.

Many of these authors have gone on to write other books afterwards, and it has led them to different career paths. As when you go through this and know the secret, you want to help others see the light, help them discover the absolute clarity and joy that comes from being alcohol free, and you can't help but share it.

So, I would recommend Quit List and Podcasts. There are so many alcohol free Podcasts now, and most of them come out on a set day and have a number of previous episodes that you can go back to. There is bound to be one that helps and inspires you. I'd recommend regularly listening to give you a different view of the ingrained messaging we've all been subjected to for years. This will help you appreciate that there is another way.

2) **Tracker**

When you first ditch the booze, tracking how many days and how much money you've saved is also helpful. I downloaded an app where I input the day I ditched drinking and wrote down my reason for wanting to ditch drinking so that I could come back to it time and time again. I also added how much money and time I spent on average daily when it came to drinking, and over time this accumulated.

I found the tracker helpful, as at the end of each day, you could note how you felt, and it would tick off the day as complete. For the first month, it tracked every day. Then it went to monthly and significant day milestones.

At each milestone, you could say the benefits you've found as well as any negatives you've experienced and see what others who have reached the same milestone have found. There was also an online community where people added their thoughts and photos, and you moved from group to group as you went further along the journey. It was always good to see familiar names getting through the milestones.

I rarely go into the app now, but I certainly found it so helpful and encouraging in my first year. It also meant I could celebrate even the smallest wins, didn't feel I was doing it alone and see how much money, in theory, I was saving by not drinking!

3) Community

Connection in the early days is so important. The likelihood is when you decide to ditch drinking for a period of time, everyone around you will still be drinking. This can make it quite challenging, especially if they are not supportive or keep tempting you to just have one. We will delve into navigating relationships in Chapter 8. However, I want to emphasise here that an alcohol free community is ready and willing to support you.

Contrary to public belief, people have made a choice to ditch drinking, not because they hit rock bottom and had to but because they knew alcohol was no longer serving them and have discovered a better life without it. One where they can be their true authentic self, they are no longer being held back or struggling to control this one thing and have experienced the benefits of being alcohol free.

So, if you are looking for inspiration, take a look at social media. There are several alcohol free groups you can join, people are posting about their journey with tips and tricks, who would love you to reach out and ask for support. This is because, once you have gone on this journey, you only want to help others see the light and join you. So, at the start, have a look around and find a community that resonates and that you can feel part of, that will support you and cheer you on. It is an amazing feeling that you want everyone to experience. You may also find alcohol free meetups in your local area that you can go to and meet like-minded people who may become lifelong friends.

4) **Delicious Alcohol Free Drinks**

For me, this was an absolute game changer, as I mentioned above. Why on earth would I continue to drink ethanol, which I know is so harmful and doesn't actually taste that great, when there is the option of an adult drink that is alcohol free? If we're being honest and think back to the taste of alcohol when we first started drinking, it wasn't pleasant.

As a teenager, I am sure, I didn't actually like the taste of alcohol, but as you feel it is the only way to transition to becoming an adult, your body gets used to it, and you learn to enjoy it.

Since I ditched drinking, the alcohol free drinks market has grown exponentially. There are so many more options now, and that's in a relatively short time. A number of millennials are now choosing not to drink, so in order to compete, companies are producing alternatives. The big alcohol brands are also now jumping on the bandwagon, as they've seen people's preferences change.

This is great for you and me, as we can experiment and find things we like. We don't have to stick to tea, coffee, water and warm orange juice, which for our inner toddler, does not work.

If we needed to just have these things, we would feel deprived and like we are missing out. But with alcohol free drinks, we can have nice drinks in adult glasses that taste good and are good for you.

You may find some of the options are quite sweet, which I don't really like, but more brands are creating options with low sugar that are gluten-free and vegan, so just look around and see what works best for you. There are so many alternatives.

If you're like me, in the beginning, you may feel like you're cheating by having alcohol free drinks. I thought, why would I do that when I said I'm not drinking for 21 days? However, for this to be sustainable, if you want to carry on longer term, having alcohol free options just makes it enjoyable, and you experience the joy of missing out. This is where you have a good night, feel like you're an adult and wake up the next day feeling great vs the fear of missing out when you feel you're depriving yourself. It's a win-win. So, try some different alternatives today.

The other thing is mocktails (alcohol free cocktails), which are great, as you can really experiment then, and if you are in a bar or restaurant and you find there are no alcohol free drinks options, you can always ask for them to make you a mocktail, as they will generally have something they can make. I've included some mocktails below for you to experiment with.

It's funny because when I go to friends' homes for dinner or a social event they may be hosting, I tend to bring alcohol free wine or fizz, just so I know I will have something that I like, but inevitably, everyone wants to try them. We went for lunch the other day, and I only brought a bottle of alcohol free wine, thinking it would only be me drinking it, and I managed to get a glass out of it. I can't complain, as it shows people are curious and open to it, but I find it strange when they then tell me how much they enjoy drinking, could never imagine not drinking and then go on to the alcoholic version. So, why drink the alcohol free version in the first place?!

If you're early days, feeling like you're white-knuckling it, as you've set yourself a 30-day challenge of not drinking and are waiting until you can have a drink and feel you're missing out, why not explore alcohol free options or host an event where you make mocktails and see if people even notice the difference! Being alcohol free does not need to be hard work, and you can keep your traditions. You just need to change what's in the glass.

Below are a few Mocktail recipes. Feel free to play around with the ingredients and make them your own.

CosNOpolitan

- 90ml Cranberry juice
- 30ml Freshly squeezed lime juice
- 60ml Sparkling water
- 30ml Orange juice

Alcohol Free Irish Cream Liqueur

- 150ml double cream
- 50ml evaporated milk
- 2 tbsp maple syrup
- 25ml freshly brewed espresso
- Pinch of ground cinnamon
- 1tsp vanilla extract
- Pinch of finely grated orange zest
- Ice

Alcohol Free Daiquiri

- 75ml white cane spirit
- 10ml vanilla syrup
- 30ml freshly squeezed lime (whole lime)
- Pinch of salt
- Lime peel
- Shake
- Add olive oil afterwards

EspressNO Martini

- 45ml white cane spirit
- 20-25ml coffee
- 30-40ml espresso (cold coffee, not hot coffee)
- Shake
    - Dry shake first without ice (this will keep the foam)
    - Then add ice and briefly shake

NOjito

- 12 to 14 small mint leaves or 6 to 7 large mint leaves
- 30ml fresh lime juice
- One tablespoon of caster sugar
- 120ml soda water
- Garnish: mint leaves, lime slices (optional)

Method

Muddle the mint leaves in a cocktail shaker with the lime juice and sugar.

Add ice cubes to fill a shaker and pour in the soda water.

Gently shake a few times to mix the ingredients. Strain into a medium or tall cocktail glass filled with ice.

Garnish, if desired.

5) **Self-Care**

When I first came across true self-care early on in my alcohol free journey, I was so surprised. I'd always thought self-care was a pampering session in a spa with a glass of champagne! However, I soon learnt that self-care was a daily occurrence of things that bring you joy, help you to relax and generally look after yourself. Most importantly, self-care does not need to be expensive.

An easy way to look at self-care is any activity you enjoy that ends with an "ing", singing, reading, baking, painting, knitting etc. There are different types of self-care, and here are a few examples:

- Physical: Exercise, Nutrition, Sleep
- Emotional: Coping Skills, Journalling, Compassion
- Social: Friends, Positive Social Media, Support System
- Spiritual: Prayer, Time Alone, Nature
- Personal: Authenticity, Creativity, Hobbies
- Space: Healthy Environment, Stability, Clean Space
- Financial: Budgeting, Money Management, Boundaries
- Work: Breaks, Time Management, Work Boundaries

Ideally, you group your self-care resources into these different categories, so depending on how you are feeling, there will be something you can do indoors or outside, and for as little or as long as you have time, in order to reset or take your mind off automatically reaching for a drink.

In December, the month after I first ditched drinking, I made a list of 21 Acts of Self-Care, which I would use as we went into the new year. This helped me focus on what I liked to do and gave me something to go back to if I was feeling bored or had time on my hands and didn't know what to do with that time.

Below is the list I came up with and regularly did throughout the year:

i. Keep a glass jar on your desk, and each week put in what you are most grateful for or proud of
ii. Exercise six days a week
iii. Drink two litres of water a day
iv. Keep a journal
v. Get into nature regularly
vi. Do things to help grow my faith
vii. Eat good food
viii. Juice
ix. Read books
x. Stay connected
xi. Switch off from phone
xii. Listen to podcasts
xiii. Do Yoga, Pilates and Barre
xiv. Paint
xv. Take photos
xvi. Say declaration every day
xvii. Bake
xviii. Master night time routine
xix. Laugh
xx. Sing and dance
xxi. Watch meaningful or enjoyable things

I hope this inspires you to create your own list and realise there is so much you can do instead of drinking and thinking about drinking!

6) Spending Time in Nature

Being alcohol free, I notice things more when I'm running or walking, bringing me back to the present, not dwelling on the past or worrying about the future.

I'm more aware of birds, butterflies, and rabbits. I even saw a muntjac deer the other day! Every day, I notice clouds and how they change. I've always been obsessed with clouds. The piece of work I submitted for my GCSE Art exam (15/16 years old) had clouds as the main theme to it. I vaguely remember it had the shape of a head and lots of clouds around it, but I can't quite remember what I was trying to create.

Anyway, I realised I had stopped paying attention, and now I make a conscious effort to notice what's around me more, and this fascinates me and gives me a sense of joy and wonder every time I look.

I notice the stars in the sky, and there are some nights I go out, look up and see the Plough, Seven Sisters, Orion's Belt and my favourite just because I loved the film Serendipity, Cassiopeia!

It's strange, but I do feel more present and aware of my surroundings, which I absolutely love that and I want you to also fully experience this. The next time you walk, run or cycle, take in your surroundings, be present and see how you feel. This was probably one of my favourite things in my alcohol free toolkit.

7) Journalling and Gratitude

Journalling is essential, especially in the early days. I found myself writing down how I was feeling and what I was experiencing a lot. This helped me to process my thoughts and feelings and reflect on whether being alcohol free was helping or hindering. At each milestone, I wrote down the benefits I'd found and how I was feeling, and this kept me going.

So, I always suggest that my clients get a journal and write down their thoughts regularly. Every morning, when you wake up, pick up your journal and write a stream of consciousness. Put pen to paper and write whatever thoughts come to mind for about three pages. You may find you can't think of anything, and if that is the case, just write, "I don't know what to write, I can't think of anything". However, you'll soon find yourself emptying what's in your head and writing.

At some point you may stop yourself just before you write something down, as you realise this is not something you want to write down or acknowledge. If this happens, you must write this down, as it may be something you need to address and deal with.

Alternatively, keep it really simple at first to get into the habit and at the end of the day, write down the answers to the three points below:

- One thing I want to remember about today
- Today, I felt...
- Today, I'm grateful for...

It is very therapeutic doing this, and there have been times when I've written things down, and then the answer I'm looking for has come to me later in the day or the next, when I am doing something else, maybe running. So, I'd recommend you buy yourself a beautiful journal and begin to write and be curious.

Gratitude helps you experience the little joys and build contentment for you to Thrive. Being grateful can help you feel more positive, improve your health and build strong relationships. I found that writing a gratitude list at the end of each day has helped me in so many ways.

I write five to ten things that have happened during the day that I've noticed, and I'm grateful for, and I try to be very specific, mindful of what it was, how I felt and what I noticed. This has helped me to feel content before I go to sleep, and it works.

Also, suppose you start to make associations with not drinking and the regular positive things that have happened during the day. In that case, you will retrain your subconscious to start to see being alcohol free as your new identity and incorporate new memories that continue to help you on your journey.

8) **Movement / Exercise**

For me, this has been running and yoga, but find some movement or exercise that you enjoy, as this helps in so many ways. I recommend trying to do something for at least 20 – 30 minutes daily.

Exercise helps in so many ways and gives you the natural highs instead of turning to alcohol to get these. You may find you already have an exercise regime you follow, which you stick with even though you feel hungover, so you already feel pretty healthy.

By ditching drinking, you'll find you enjoy this even more. Like me, you won't find yourself doing a lower back stretch feeling nauseous or headachy or pushing yourself, knowing you'd had too much to drink the night before but feeling guilty if you don't stick to your routine.

Exercise becomes so much more enjoyable, no longer feels like a chore, and you get more out of it.

So, now you understand what an Alcohol Free Toolkit is. I hope you think about developing one for yourself, as these are practical things you can do that will make being alcohol free sustainable and enjoyable.

A final tool I wanted to share is HALT. When you want to reach for that drink or hear the wine witch or something whisper, you need a drink, pause and think HALT. Know that cravings are just thoughts, and they, too, shall pass. So, as you go to get your favourite tipple, ask yourself, "Am I feeling":

- **H**UNGRY? Eat! Have some good nutritious food.
- **A**NGRY? Move, shake, punch a cushion, run, let it out!
- **L**ONELY? Get connected and share how you're feeling with your alcohol free community.
- **T**IRED? Have a nap, breathe deeply or just go to sleep!

Bonus: "Am I feeling FEARFUL?" Go for a walk, breathe, have a cup of tea, take a bath, visualise a happy place, talk to someone, and challenge the thought!

If you challenge your beliefs on alcohol and think HALT each time you'd like a drink, you will soon find you no longer need alcohol, it will no longer be part of your automatic thought pattern, and you will finally be able to ditch drinking.

Questions to ask yourself:

1. What are you struggling with at the moment?
2. Based on what you've read in this chapter, what could help you with the struggle(s)?
3. What one thing can you do today?

Action:

- Create an alcohol free toolkit that you can go to whenever you feel like you want a drink.

A Cocktail of Clarity Concept

Tip: "Next time you reach for a drink, ask yourself, what feeling am I escaping from or trying to create? Then think, is there something else I can do instead?" @thrivealcoholfree

> We drink to create a feeling, e.g. we want to feel relaxed, less anxious or more sophisticated. We're trying to escape from reality or issues going on in life.
>
> Before you reach for a glass, pause and think about the feeling and go for a walk in nature, do some exercise or eat something. Then go back and

question if you still need a drink. It's amazing what the pause can do.

FIRSTS

Embody a New Alcohol Free Identity

Chapter 7:
The First Hurdle

"If you're serious about changing your life, you'll find a way. If you're not, you'll find an excuse."

Jen Sincero

They say the best time to plant a tree was ten years ago. However, the next best time is today, so why wait to ditch drinking? If you've had enough, been thinking alcohol is no longer serving you or just feel that life could be better without it, then start today. You won't regret it! If you're afraid that by ditching drinking, you'll be bored, miss out, won't be able to do it, or your family and friends may think that you're strange, then just know this chapter will help you.

How do I get through my first alcohol free event? This is a question that I'm asked all the time. When you are so used to having alcohol on every occasion, you feel lost, not knowing what to do with yourself, as you get used to your shiny new alcohol free shoes.

This chapter will cover some of the alcohol firsts you may go through, and I will give examples of how I managed to get through these in my own life. At the end of the chapter, I will introduce you to one tool that will become your go-to when you enter any new situation. I still use this today, even though it's no longer an alcohol thing, as it can be applied to how you want to feel before any important event, meeting or social do.

When you ditch drinking, the benefits are amazing, but it can leave you feeling out of sorts, not quite yourself, and every new activity can make you feel uneasy. You may also find even though you are in the situation, it feels like you are watching from above and observing yourself and others, as this new person is not who you are used to being.

This is all perfectly normal, and everyone experiences something similar in the early days or when they have a major alcohol free first, such as a birthday, holiday or work event. This is what keeps people stuck for so long. I remember thinking if I wanted to stop drinking for a month, I would look ahead and say, but I have a big party or a wedding coming up, or there's a conference/networking event I need to attend, or I'm travelling for work, so how could I stop now, it would be far too inconvenient, and you never get started. There will always be something coming up. This is why, if you feel alcohol is no longer serving you, and you want to have a break, you just have to bite the bullet and go for it, as there will never be a good or right time.

So, what do alcohol free firsts look like, and how do you get through them? Here are five tips that will help in all situations:

1. **Find Alcohol Free Alternatives**
   The alcohol free drinks market has expanded so much in the past couple of years that there are plenty of options out there. You just have to find the ones you like. You can pretty much find an alternative to all the drinks that you may have

enjoyed before, plus there are many more to try, and they taste great!

I know for some people, alcohol free drinks may be triggering, but a cup of tea at a party won't hack it, as your inner toddler will feel like they're missing out, so I'd suggest at least having something in a nice grown-up glass that makes you feel like you are not missing out. You can get sparkling tea, kombucha or an artisan tonic, which may be a better alternative for you.

2. **Prep Ahead and Know What To Say**

    If you are going to a social event, go online and check what alcohol free options the bar or restaurant has. If there aren't any, think about what you can have instead, e.g. soda and lime, flavoured tonic water or make a note of mocktail ingredients that you can ask for when you arrive.

    If you are going to someone's house but are not ready to get into a conversation about what you're doing, then bring your own alcohol free drinks. When people ask you why you're not drinking, have a reason prepared, and this can be anything from "I'm driving", "I'm trying to be healthier", "I have an early start", etc. You are under no obligation to explain yourself.

    Don't worry; most people won't even mention it once they've had their first drink. Alternatively, ask them a question about themselves to change the subject if they do continue to question you!

3. **Practice Self-Care**
   As part of your alcohol free toolkit, it's important you have things you can go to when the cravings come or if you feel you need to step away from any uncomfortable situation. Think about things that make you happy, which are your go-to self-care activities.

   You may want to go for a run or walk first thing before the event, or if you are away for a weekend with friends, you could take yourself off to listen to a podcast or do some yoga at some point in the day or plan to do something like a jigsaw or knitting while people are drinking or there is some down time. However, make sure you've thought of a few activities, just in case you can't do the ideal one. For example, it may not be possible to go for a 5k run while you're in the middle of dinner, but you could play your favourite music to boost your mood or just breathe.

4. **Plan Something The Morning After**
   When you have a night out planned, if you feel tempted to have a drink, play it forward. What would happen if you had that drink, where would it lead, and how would you feel the next day?

   If you have something fun planned for the morning, this will also give you motivation to not drink and can hold you accountable.

5. **Own Your Alcohol Free Identity**
   Be proud of where you are on your alcohol free journey and how far you've come, regardless of the

number of days you've been alcohol free. Not many people can do what you're doing, so it is a great achievement! As you go through the event, remember your why, think about all the things you're gaining and own your new identity.

Finally, if this is something you've chosen to do, see it as a non-negotiable and enjoy the process. How great will it be to think you have got through the event and not wavered!

Below are some common situations you may find yourself in and will hopefully give you some ideas on how to Thrive Alcohol Free.

Socialising

> The first time we went for a meal with our good friends, I felt quite nervous. We had only ever socialised with drinks, and that had been since day one, so I couldn't imagine what it would be like if I wasn't drinking and I stressed about it. I thought about how to get out of it or leave early if I needed to and what I needed to take with me to make sure I didn't feel like I was missing out.
>
> My biggest fear was that I wouldn't enjoy their company and I would be bored. However, I realised I liked them and could still laugh without drinking! They were supportive, although they did ask things like, are you stopping forever or just a little while? But that was fair enough, and I was probably only a month in at the time, and I didn't know the answer to that, but I did know I saw benefits, and I

remember feeling relieved that I could socialise without it!

Networking Events

Networking events, such as conferences is an area I'd love to see having more choices for people who are alcohol free. I've been to several networking events since I ditched drinking and don't understand why the only option, other than red wine or white wine, is warm orange juice! If you don't fancy sweet, tangy orange juice, water is the only other option. Even though several restaurants and bars have now started to provide alcohol free options in their menus, the catering industry for these types of events still seems to be way behind the curve.

It would be nice to be given the option of an alcohol free drink, as many people at these events opt for red wine or white wine and, in some of the fancier ones, a glass of fizz. So, when you're drinking water, it can feel like you stand out, and you tend to keep being offered red or white wine, as if to say why are you only drinking water!

I want to encourage you, by letting you know, you are not odd if you decide you no longer want to drink. I mean, you can't go anywhere now without having a vegetarian option. You're not going to force someone to either eat meat or alternatively starve! This should be the same for people who choose not to drink alcohol, and they should get a choice of something alcohol free that isn't water.

Anyway, when you are at these events with no other option, please don't worry about what people are thinking, as it is mainly in your head, especially if it is your first alcohol free experience. In general, people don't notice or ask, as it is likely the first time they have met you. Contrary to public belief, you can stand and talk to someone without a glass in hand, but if that makes you feel uncomfortable, you could put the water in a wine glass, if this helps psychologically.

I was at an event recently, and I was happily chatting to people when someone I came over and said, can I get you a drink, which was thoughtful, but I asked what there was, and of course, it was immediately, there is a lovely alcoholic beverage and another, so I just said, "I'll have a glass of water, thanks."

It will get to the point where you feel comfortable in your alcohol free identity to not care. Trust me and trust the process. You will feel so happy in your new skin that it won't bother you.

If you are reading this and work in the catering industry for conferences and events, please suggest, to people in your sphere of influence, that alcohol free drinks would be much appreciated! Thanks.

Work Dinner

My first work dinner, which happened to be my leaving do, was the first in-person get-together with people from work since before COVID, and they didn't know I wasn't drinking, so I was quite nervous. In hindsight, it may have been useful to tell at least one person.

I was the first to arrive, and when the next person arrived, they asked if I'd like a gin & tonic, as that was what I was known for drinking. When I said no thanks, they looked at me very strangely. I think they thought I might be pregnant or something! I had seen the menu and said I'd have something non-alcoholic.

As we were at a steak restaurant, red wine was a given, so when I said to another colleague I wasn't drinking red wine, they seemed shocked and immediately told me of someone they knew who had hit rock bottom during COVID! This insinuated that I must have a problem if I wasn't drinking, which can be a ridiculous conclusion that some people come to. However, please know that you do not need to defend yourself or get into a conversation about it if you don't want to. It's none of their business, and the fact you have made a conscious decision not to ever get to that point is wonderful. Remember that. It also says more about them than it does about you. Anyway, I made it clear, it just wasn't serving me, and there was no scandalous story and moved the conversation on.

Listening to the conversations, I realised why I was leaving and was just bored. I was beginning to think, why had I bothered to come and I should have known it would annoy me, however, I told myself I needed to be grateful, as it was kind of them to do this for me. Then the most random thing happened, a magician saved me. Yes, you read this correctly, a magician, of all things changed the night for me, and I thoroughly enjoyed it. The point here is to look for things that can make a night enjoyable that are not booze related or feel free to leave early. You are allowed.

Holiday

My first holiday after I stopped drinking was a short break where we had a house on the lake in the Cotswolds and were going with good friends of ours and their two children. We had been on holiday together a few times, which normally involved drinking. So, this time would be different, but luckily, I was able to prep. I took AF drinks, planned to run, as I had a 10k race coming up, and thought about enjoying the jacuzzi and the lake. It was fine. We had such a laugh. I love how I genuinely laugh now, and it is belly laughing, tears rolling down your eyes type of laugh that feels so good!

My first holiday abroad felt like a bigger deal, as it was our first one since COVID, and we were going to an All Inclusive resort. This triggered thoughts, such as one of the main perks of All Inclusive was drinking, so why would you go on an All Inclusive holiday if you weren't going to drink? What else could you do? I was nearly 18 months into my AF journey, so although I felt comfortable in my alcohol free identity, I didn't know what to expect, as all my previous holidays as an adult involved drinking.

However, I had nothing to worry about, as it was one of the best holidays. We went to bed early and got up early. We'd go for a lovely family walk in the morning along the beach when it was quiet, although a few early risers and runners also made the most of the start of the day. This surprised me so much, and I realised I'd been missing out all this time. Who knew, as generally I'd be asleep, then wake up feeling foggy, go for a late breakfast and then feel the only way to get rid of the head was to start drinking again, what a waste! So, it is absolutely true when I say you are only gaining.

On the first evening, we arrived, though, I had water, as when I asked for an alcohol free option, they looked at me very strangely. So, I thought that would be it and gave myself a pep talk, thought about my WOOP (I'll go into this later in the chapter) and said I'd be fine with tea, coffee, water and juice if needed, but I was determined to enjoy it.

Anyway, the next day, bless him, my Husband asked if there was anything at the bar that they could make that was alcohol free, and the NOjito became my friend for the rest of the trip. It was my go-to drink, and it felt like a grown-up drink, so it didn't give my inner child a chance to feel that something wasn't right based on all my previous memories and the associations my brain automatically goes to when it comes to vacations. It's amazing; even 18 months in, you can still wobble. Someone recently talked about a similar thing. They were alcohol free for over two years but had felt triggered on holiday, so something to be aware of.

On this holiday, we watched the shows they put on and had such a fab time. Again, I laughed so hard at one of the events. We ate some wonderful food, watched the sunset, and enjoyed time getting soaked on the lazy river, another funny experience. All in all, it was such a fun holiday.

What struck me, though, was that I wanted to come home once the holiday was finished. I was looking forward to coming home. I realised I loved this new alcohol free life that I'd created, and I was no longer escaping from it, which I think a lot of people do when they go on holiday. It's the main thing they look forward to, and when they head home, they dread what will hit them when they hit the tarmac. This could be because of the alcohol and the fact it exacerbates anxiety, stress and depression or that they are not living the life they really want. Or, who knows, maybe a combination of both.

If you're about to go on holiday or just want to try it, go back and make a note of the Nojito recipe in Chapter 6, it's fab!

Wedding

Another event that many people feel they need to drink at is a wedding. If you have a wedding coming up, the last thing you'd want to do is not be drinking at this time. They can be awkward. You may only know the bride and groom and a couple of others, so you are forced to mingle with strangers. Weddings are also long days, and there is a lot of hanging around waiting for photos to be taken and in between the wedding breakfast and the evening event, so most people find drinking in this situation is a must and of course, it's a celebration, so toasting with a glass of fizz is a given!

Again, I ask you to consider whether this is absolutely true. Is everyone drinking at weddings? Can you enjoy a wedding and dance(?!) without a drink? How have you felt the morning after previous weddings?

The first wedding I went to after ditching drinking, I was a little apprehensive. However, I did prep and took a couple of alcohol free bottles with me. At the wedding breakfast, I drank my AF red wine at the table. I didn't make a fuss and doubt anyone noticed. It was a table full of strangers, as I didn't know anyone other than the bride and groom. I was really there to keep my husband company.

The interesting thing I realised was when I looked around. It seemed like a very dry do. People didn't seem to be knocking back the wine. Prior to ditching drinking, I thought that by the time we sat down for the wedding breakfast, I would definitely have had a few drinks, would have felt I could chat to people about anything and would continue to drink at the table. But when I looked around, it seemed very tame. I don't know if I was more aware or if it was because it was a wedding with people I'd never met, so not my usual friends who drank.

However, then the rum came out! As part of the wedding breakfast, they put on rum tasting, which people did fully partake in. Rum was the last thing I wanted, and I realised I wasn't in any way tempted by it.

So, this made me think maybe it's just different, and people still enjoy a drink at weddings. It did give me food for thought, though, as although we may believe it to be true and it is ingrained in our society that a wedding equals piss up, it is actually possible to attend a wedding and not drink alcohol!

Birthday

If, like me, you have always celebrated your birthday with champagne. The very first one can feel quite strange. I was nearly six months into my alcohol free journey when I celebrated my first alcohol free birthday, and as I was now used to alcohol free fizz, this was the obvious substitute. However, I found I wanted to go for a run first thing and start my new year that way. I also wanted to do my morning and evening routine! I realised I had the tools in place, alcohol was no longer important, and I wanted to celebrate in other ways. I thoroughly enjoyed the meal and the cake. I spent it with my family and enjoyed time with them, and I had no need to have a big get-together with lots of people.

It was just chilled. If you have a birthday earlier in the journey and it causes you to wobble, go back to the five tips above and remember your why. The older you get, the more detrimental to your health alcohol becomes, so just think, by being alcohol free, you are hopefully helping your health and wellbeing for your future self.

Business Travel

If you travel for business, you may, like me, feel nervous about doing this without alcohol. Again, it sounds ridiculous to me now, but as soon as you get to the airport, alcohol is on offer, and then you tend to socialise to get to know the people you are working with better and of course, that has to involve drinking. So, although you are working hard, you certainly end up playing hard too.

Sitting on a plane back from my third abroad business trip, I found myself watching the trolly cart and reflecting on alcohol. This business trip felt quite different to my first. I was watching the trolly cart and realised that everyone still drinks. This may sound surprising, but I have surrounded myself with an alcohol free community and a number of people I follow and listen to are alcohol free. I forget that this is uncommon.

The majority of people asked for red wine, white wine, and fizz (champagne) with their lunch. I watched a man ask about the wine choices and looked like he was quite the connoisseur, very proud of that fact and seemed to think the red wine he selected was appropriate.

The thought that came to mind was how comfortable I felt in my alcohol free skin and how with all the knowledge I have now, I felt like saying to everyone, "Do you know how life could be so much better without alcohol?" or "you really don't need to drink this toxic substance to enjoy a flight?". My next thought was, how glad I was to have seen the light. The scales had well and truly come off, and I wanted that for everyone else.

Earlier, I had literally just boarded the plane, putting my things in the overhead storage, when the host said to me, "I don't mean to disturb you, but I didn't want you to miss out on the fabulous drinks. We have this sparkling rose…" and I said, I don't drink. He looked a little shocked/sorry for me, and it made me smile. A couple of years ago, I may have questioned more and asked myself, am I missing it?

Should I be drinking, but I was no longer in that place? I had grown, learnt and become a version of myself that knew that alcohol would not give me anything, and it was a choice. I could drink, but I choose not to, and I was not going to get off the plane dehydrated with jet lag. As it may come as a surprise to you but alcohol dehydrates and does not help in any way with jet lag. Since I've ditched drinking, I've not suffered from jet lag.

I'm not writing this to be judgemental or say look at me but to show that in the early days when you are faced with alcohol firsts, it seems like everything takes more effort. You need to prep, you need to do your WOOP and have an alcohol free alternative that keeps your inner child from spitting out the dummy, but as you go through these firsts, you learn, you grow, and you don't think about it. It is no longer an issue.

Before becoming alcohol free, I would have been the one having champagne on the flight. What was the purpose of business class without having a glass of champagne when you first get on the plane?! I would then have a gin & tonic as an aperitif and then red wine with the meal. The joy of flying was drinking, but in hindsight, I realise now that it was not helping me in any way.

This trip had been great; again, it made me realise how different I was. In addition to a productive work week, meeting people face-to-face, who I'd been speaking to on Zoom for so long, I also made sure I stuck to my morning and evening routines, which helped me to intentionally spend my free time in an enjoyable way. I spent time in the word, meditated and had my green juice and ginger shot in the mornings. I did yoga in the evenings. I ran on the treadmill in the fitness centre and made sure I was intentional about how I spent my time, and practised self-care, which helped me be my best during the week.

When I previously travelled, there was no intentionality from a self-care perspective. It was a work hard, play hard mentality and now, as I think about it, I realise, it was these weeks of travelling, sometimes every week for months, that gave me the habit of drinking most days and then every day, as that was just what you did. You're offered alcohol on the plane. In the good old days, as a member of a hotel, there were complimentary drinks in the members' lounge, you'd go for dinner, and wine was a must, and then wake up work until late and do the same thing again. Of course, my tolerance must have developed over time, and it just became normal, so I can't say I felt it affected my work, but gosh, now I know I could have been on absolute fire if I'd ditched drinking earlier, but the thought never crossed my mind, and I suppose, I wanted to fit in and keep up with the rest of the team, as this was the done thing.

If you travel for work regularly and are using this as another reason not to ditch drinking, have a think about this. Is it true that you need to drink to get through a business trip?

Christmas & New Year

It may seem impossible to stay alcohol free during this festive season. Alcohol seems to be everywhere during this time. When you walk through the entrance of supermarkets, it's the first thing you see, it's on adverts everywhere and featured in Christmas movies/tv shows, and it seems everyone is drinking at every social gathering you attend!

However, if you think about what you want and how you'd like the season to go for you, plus what could get in the way of you achieving that and have a plan for these obstacles, then you will no doubt get to the first of January alcohol free and set yourself up in the best way for the New Year! You will then, no doubt, go from strength to strength as you experience that being alcohol free is actually a superpower and the best-kept secret!

I'd only ditched the booze for a short space of time. I was less than two months in when I hit my first alcohol free Christmas, having initially only planned to stop drinking for 21 days. I remember thinking there was no way I could get through Christmas and New Year alcohol free, and I fully expected it to be a bit of a challenge.

How would I cope without partaking in our normal traditions on Christmas Day, which, when I thought about it, seemed to mainly revolve around alcohol? I think that's because it's the one day of the year you are allowed to overindulge.

For me, that meant no champagne with my smoked salmon breakfast, no champagne and red wine with the turkey dinner, no port after dinner, no baileys coffee or a nightcap!

Christmas comes with so many traditions and associations that go back to when we were children, and so if you've been drinking for a while, a lot of memories around Christmas probably involved alcohol. I can totally relate to this, as my first alcohol free Christmas was the only one I'd had as an adult, other than being pregnant with our daughter.

However, as the days went on and Christmas was approaching, I learned there was an alternative way, and the benefits outweighed anything I thought I might miss out on, so I embraced the challenge and prepped ahead to ensure I was able to manage. It was also a good opportunity to try a selection of new alcohol free drinks!

I remember wrapping gifts on Christmas Eve with alcohol free mulled wine (I have a delicious recipe for that if you're interested!) and waking up on Christmas morning eager to see our daughter's face, as she excitedly discovered that Santa had been. Watching her unwrap gifts and then going through the day fully present, taking things in and noticing more than I normally would was wonderful. It was a fantastic Christmas, and I discovered it is absolutely possible to celebrate alcohol free!

A tool that I've referred to in this chapter and have found extremely helpful and personally continue to use in different situations even now is WOOP. For any event, go through a WOOP, which is your:

- **W**ISH: What do you wish the alcohol free event will be like
- **O**UTCOME: How do you want to feel / what do you want to have achieved afterwards?
- **OB**STACLE: What could stop you from achieving your wish and outcome?
- **P**LAN: How can you prepare / what plan can you put in place to avoid the obstacle?

Before any event or situation, write down your WOOP. Alternatively, once you get used to the concept, you can think it through in your mind. By doing this, you are effectively setting your intention, which subconsciously will allow you to at least move towards that intention. I have done this several times now, and most recently, I did it for a business trip on a plane. On my way home, I returned to it and realised I'd achieved my wish and outcomes and avoided the obstacles with the plan.

Clients I've worked with have found this to be a highly useful tool. In addition to alcohol free firsts, I've seen them use it to define what a one-month break from drinking would look like, and it helps them really think about what they want to achieve. It also has encouraged them to focus on staying alcohol free and enjoying the journey, as they realised they can get through situations they once thought would have been impossible.

I do believe we overthink and anticipate alcohol free events far more than we need to, and if there is an awkward moment or someone is pushing us to have a drink, we must remember we are in control, and there is a reason we have decided to ditch drinking, so let's be comfortable with that decision, make sure we're prepared and enjoy it! You are still fun, you can still make conversation, and you are more than capable of thriving in any alcohol free situation. You just need to believe in yourself, remember you are doing an amazing thing and smile knowing you have a superpower!

Questions to ask yourself:

1. What is an alcohol free first you have coming up, and based on what you've read, how can you prepare for it?
2. Ask yourself, "What do I want this alcohol free first to be like?" Then ask, "How do I have to be in order for that to be like that? Finally, ask, "What support and resources do I need?"
3. How can you play forward in your mind the next day? If you were to drink, how would it feel? If you stayed alcohol free, how would it feel?

Action:

- If you have an alcohol free first or a social event coming up this week, develop a WOOP (Wish, Outcome, Obstacle, Plan) to help you prepare.

A Cocktail of Clarity Concept

Fascination: "Thinking about how you would manage alcohol free first is one reason you may not want to stop drinking... consider which alcohol free first you would find most challenging." @thrivealcoholfree

> I've been alcohol free for nearly two years, and I think one of the reasons it took me so long to ditch the booze was wondering how to deal with various events that I'd always associated with drinking. But once I got through some of these alcohol free firsts,

I realised choosing to be alcohol free was the best decision I could have made.

Questions you may be asking yourself are how do I socialise without booze? How do I celebrate without it? How do I commiserate without it? How do I fit in without it? Will I ever dance again without alcohol?!!!

Are you questioning your relationship with alcohol but feeling stuck, as you can't imagine life without it? You're not the first person to think that.

Over the past two years, I've gone through most alcohol free firsts, but last month I had an alcohol free first, and I did have a moment where I thought this could be interesting. But in the end, there was nothing to be worried about.

If you're thinking about ditching the booze but are not sure where to start and looking for additional support, feel free to get in touch.

Chapter 8:
It's Not About Them

"Our deepest fear is not that we are inadequate; our deepest fear is that we are powerful beyond measure. It is our light, not our darkness, that frightens us."
Nelson Mandela

When people consider ditching drinking, even for a short period of time, a number of them get stuck and decide not to take the step, as they worry about what others will think. This then becomes a stumbling block, and many never get started.

If, like I was, you are a people pleaser, you may think you will be disappointing someone if you don't drink or even though you really don't fancy a drink, you say yes, so as not to offend! It's fairly ridiculous when you see this written in black and white!

Well, enough is enough. This really isn't about them; it's about you, your life and the amazing future you are stopping yourself from stepping into. So, this chapter will hopefully help answer the question, how do I navigate my relationships with family and friends that drink?

In the beginning, when you are not used to being alcohol free, I admit it is uncomfortable, and you start to notice things about people you've known for years that you've maybe ignored or used alcohol to numb out your true feelings towards them.

You may have friends you realise aren't really friends and you have nothing in common with them other than drinking, which can be a bit of a shock at first. This may eventually mean you grow apart. You may also get people you least expect to start questioning your choices and try to convince you to continue drinking. This says more about them than it does about you, and the likelihood is you are holding up a mirror to them and their relationship with alcohol.

I'm convinced many people would love to ditch drinking but have such strong beliefs about what alcohol does for them or could never imagine fitting into society without it that they shy away from questioning it and just have another drink to drown out any thoughts of there potentially being a different way!

So, in the early days, I suggest you don't make a big deal of it and maybe only tell one or two people you are doing this, feel free to get in touch and let me know if you like. However, you can be as vague or detailed as you want and choose to be with family and friends. You could tell your Partner, "I'm doing a health challenge, so I won't drink for the next 30 days. Please support me on this." Or be honest and say, "I am not drinking for 30 days, as alcohol is making me feel anxious and tired (fill in the blank), and I need to have a break from it."

For your friendship group, if you need to let them know, keep any explanation brief or just say, "I'm not drinking tonight, as I'm on antibiotics, I'm driving, whatever reason you feel comfortable with", and quickly change the subject, "How was your week?"

I certainly would not try to argue, defend or justify your actions, as any doubt they see in you may convince them to try to get you to have a drink. As you become more secure in your new alcohol free shoes, you will be more confident, and when asked if you want a drink, you'll probably say, "I'd love a lime & soda" or "An alcohol free gin and tonic would be amazing, thanks!" Then if someone questions why you don't drink, the likelihood is, you won't bat an eyelid and will confidently be able to say, "I feel so good now that I'm not drinking. I've realised I don't need to drink" and leave it at that, as how can anyone argue with you feeling good"!

It's such a shame that in our society, alcohol is the only drug you need to justify not taking! Would someone turn around to you and say, "Go on, surely you can have a little bit of cocaine!" Ok, maybe a bit extreme, but they also wouldn't say to a vegan at a BBQ, "Go on, have a beefburger!" No, they wouldn't, so why is it such a challenge for people to say they are not drinking and feel so pressured when they have made a choice? It's because drinking is so socially acceptable and the adult thing to do. People can't understand why you wouldn't!

Suppose you are early on your alcohol free journey or even well into it. In that case, you are allowed to set boundaries, and you can say "No" to things that you feel will trigger you or that you simply don't want to do, as you no longer find them enjoyable. If you do attend a social event with friends, in addition to doing your WOOP before you go, make sure you have an exit strategy, and if you find you are an hour in and just want to go home, feel free to slip away, most people won't notice or question it, but you can celebrate that you went and go home, make yourself a herbal tea and read your book in bed if that is what you want to do. Do not add any additional pressure on yourself, as you don't need to.

Finally, when it comes to socialising and doing things with friends that may revolve around drinking and the word "should" pops into your head, "I should or ought to do this because…", ask yourself who says you should and why should you? You will soon realise it is you putting this on yourself, as you shouldn't have to do anything you don't want to. Setting boundaries is healthy, and the stronger you become in your alcohol free identity, the more you will be able to set those boundaries and not worry about what people think. Remember, it's not about them!

The main concern clients mention is what will happen to their closest relationship if they don't drink. Many have been with their Partner for years when they decide to give being alcohol free a go, making them question their decision. They met their Partner over drinks. Then continued to do life together with drinks. They socialise with friends and family with drinks, go on date nights where having a meal with wine is just what they do, celebrate & commiserate with drinks, go on holiday and have cocktails, visit vineyards and go wine tasting together. Pretty much their whole relationship revolves around alcohol, and this can be tough.

My husband and I had been together for 20 years when I made the decision to ditch drinking. We have grown up, gone through life and seen our fair share of highs & lows together. When I reflect on this, drinking had always been part of our lives, and it was only when I was pregnant that I didn't drink; to be supportive, he didn't drink much. This was certainly one of the things I worried about in the early days, even when I said I'd only do 21 days.

I told him I was ditching drinking for a while, and he was incredibly supportive. At no point did he make me feel I was doing anything weird or make me feel I should be drinking. When I discovered alcohol free drinks, we just kept the ritual and changed the ingredients, so he would have a gin & tonic, and I would have an alcohol free gin & tonic. He even helped me make alcohol free cocktails and backed all the new things I was trying.

I know this isn't the case for everyone, and I am aware that Partners may feel judged or worry that you might change and wonder how this could affect the relationship, but that is where the alcohol free community comes in.

However, there is no need to sugar-coat it. The beginning does feel odd. Your body is recalibrating. You're potentially not sleeping as well. You are feeling out of sorts and wondering if it is all worth it, and on top of that may find yourself getting irritated or frustrated that all your Partner seems to do is drink!

At the time, I thought to myself, "I don't want to drink for now, and so I will need to find other things to do in the evenings after our daughter is in bed." I've been there and done that. It probably wasn't the case, but I was hypersensitive, and as I found more time on my hands, gained clarity and had more focus, the last thing I wanted to do was sit and watch TV, I wanted to do things that were more meaningful, and I think this is where my passion for reading, doing courses, self-care and personal growth really started to develop.

Fast forward to just after me being alcohol free for two years, my Husband decided he no longer wanted to drink and has not done so since, which is unbelievable! For a while, I felt we no longer had much in common, and I could feel myself growing and wanting more. However, little did I know I may have been inspiring him over time.

It's really important to surround yourself with like-minded people who have made the same choice and are going through or slightly ahead of where you are, as they can help you navigate the journey. The likelihood is they will also have experiences they can share.

Another challenge people face is that when they ditch drinking, they don't want alcohol in the house as it triggers them, and they worry it might tempt them, but their Partner was still drinking. So, in these cases, I suggest asking your Partner to put the alcohol bottles somewhere else to where it usually is, either in another cupboard or in the garage for example. Also, if your Partner is not supportive, you may be shining a light on them, which they may be sensitive to.

Becoming alcohol free is a choice. However, it's a hard choice when you look around, and your friends, family, and society say that drinking is the norm. I still get asked if I miss it or wish I was drinking when I'm in a bar or a restaurant with friends or colleagues, and I get this look that says you know you are missing out.

It's interesting because every now and again, something (the wine witch) tries to say enough is enough now. You've done so well, but surely you want to drink now?!

In these situations, I could choose to listen to this or question it and reflect on whether it's true. The truth is you don't need alcohol to live life, and alcohol does not help you to be your most authentic self, live your best life and reach your full potential. It, in fact, does quite the opposite.

If I look back over the time that I've been alcohol free, so many wonderful things have happened, doors have opened, I am a better person, as I've grown in so many ways, I have more clarity and know no benefits come from drinking.

It's not about ditching the booze. It's always about what comes next, the unexpected things that happen and how you feel, plus the tools and habits you put in place that allow you to be who you want to become and live the life you are supposed to live.

Don't focus on what you think you're achieving by choosing to live differently but focus on who you want to become and then pick habits and a community that will help you get there.

Even though you may think it's hard or not to have support, remember you are doing this for yourself. You can never make such a huge lifestyle change for anyone else apart from you; everyone has their own journey. Life is too short to worry about what others think, and you have too much to do. Your purpose and wonderful future are waiting for you on the other side, where you will no doubt inspire others, and they may even eventually join you on this beautiful alcohol free journey. If this is something you want to do, you need to be clear on your why, make it a non-negotiable and trust the process.

Questions to ask yourself:
1. Remind yourself, what is your why for ditching drinking?
2. Who are you most worried about when it comes to not drinking, and what is the reason?
3. What could you do to make you both feel comfortable with your decision?

Action:

- Think about what your response will be when people ask you about not drinking. (It can be as long or as short as you like!)

A Cocktail of Clarity Concept

Tip: "Don't worry about other people's opinions if you decide to ditch drinking." @thrivealcoholfree

You may be really keen to take a break from alcohol, but you feel stuck as you worry about what others will think.

If you and your partner have always had drinks together, you may feel nervous about what it could mean if you didn't drink for a while. Would you get the support you need? Will it drive a wedge between them? Will you still have things in common?

Or you may go out with the girls every other week, and what would that mean, as that always involves having a glass of fizz or two?

You may be stopping yourself from doing the one thing that has been niggling you for ages because you want to please people or are afraid they will think you're boring.

If this is the case, reflect on this today. How could your life change for the better if you ditched drinking? Would you feel less anxious? Will you have more energy? Will you have more clarity?

Whatever reason you come up with, think about whether it's worth not trying just to please others and make a choice. You will know what's best for you. Just remember, though, it's not about them.

Chapter 9:
Where's The Passion

"Am I living in a way that's deeply satisfying and truly expresses me?"

Carl Rodgers

Have you lost your passion? If you're honest with yourself, you may be thinking I don't know what I'm passionate about, or how do I find out what I'm passionate about? Are you wondering if there is anything you're truly passionate about and what last sparked you?

When I look back, I realise I had lost my passion when I found myself brought to tears by the film "The Greatest Showman"! Ok, if you're currently chuckling or thinking, what is she on about? Bear with me.

If you've seen the film, I'd like to think you'd agree it's probably one of the best modern musicals of its time, but maybe you weren't brought to tears. If you haven't seen it, first, watch it, but as you won't do that now, I'll give you a synopsis. It's about a boy who loses his father at a young age and has to find his own way. As a young man, he has a big dream, of wanting to start a circus and marry the daughter of a wealthy family his father used to work for. He is constantly striving to prove himself so that he fits in. He wants to impress people and make his far-fetched idea come to fruition.

Along the way, he and the rest of the cast go through trials and tribulations with fantastic songs about identity, love, and moving onwards and upwards. I remember watching it the first time, being completely engrossed and wondering what would happen. Seeing the passion this man had to do what seemed impossible was heart-warming, and I thought what an amazing film and the tears rolled down my face.

One of the songs is all about the impossible coming true, and everything you ever want and need is there in front of you, and you're where you want to be. Another one talks about coming alive and dreaming with your eyes wide open. At the time, I didn't know what impossible thing I wanted to achieve. I didn't know what I wanted; if I was honest, I had lost myself and stopped dreaming.

On reflection, I now know I cried because I wasn't passionate about anything then. I wanted to find something I was passionate about and wanted to make a difference in the world. When you ditch drinking, you start to see the world in technicolour, and you come alive! I believe so many people are living in a world that is a bit grey. That isn't the world they want to live in, as they know deep down there is more.

I've seen the film a few times since and still find it inspiring, but I can honestly say that since ditching drinking, I've found many passions and am fully living again.

With more clarity, awareness and time on my hands, I started to think about what I enjoyed doing. They say passions are inside you, but if you have been drinking for a while, you may have forgotten what you are passionate about and struggle to work out your passions.

I have rediscovered passions I'd forgotten I enjoyed and found new ones. I also notice a lot more around me, either in nature or being more aware of the people around me. When you ditch alcohol, a light seems to go on, which has been lost.

I was speaking to someone the other day and asked: "If you had 15 minutes to yourself, what you would do?" The person couldn't think of anything. I believe alcohol dims the bright light inside you and stops you from fully living the wonderful fun adventure that life is.

If you've ditched drinking, how are you feeling? I imagine you might find that you suddenly feel you have more time. It's interesting because I think when you are drinking, you are constantly thinking about drinking. So, you are thinking, do I have a drink? Don't I have a drink? Shall I have a drink today? I didn't feel great yesterday, so maybe I won't have a drink. But if I have a drink, what am I going to have? Or I'm going here, and what will I have to drink?

It can become just something that's in your head constantly, and you don't even realise it's there. So, when you are a few weeks in not drinking, you might be feeling a little bit bored.

I remember I felt a bit bored. I felt there was a lot of time, and I wasn't sure what to do with the time and how to make the most of it. We don't realise that many of our passions, hobbies, and things we enjoy doing, even just tiny things, such as noticing our surroundings more and being fully present in the moment, have disappeared. Since ditching drinking, I really notice more around me, such as the formations of clouds and leaves in the trees. Seeing rabbits and muntjac deer on my runs and taking a lot more in. Having clarity, more awareness, and then actually taking the time to think about what I want to do with my time never gets old.

There are still 24 hours in the day and 1,444 minutes. That hasn't changed. It's just I'm more intentional about how I use my time and what I do with it.

What do you do with that time? You have 24 hours every day. Let's say you work eight hours. You sleep eight hours. What are you doing with the rest of the eight hours? I really encourage you to think about what your passions are, what your hobbies are and how you really want to spend your time. Be intentional.

You may be thinking. I don't really know what my passions are because I haven't really thought about them. If this is the case, why not think back to when you were a child and think about what you liked doing when you were younger? Would you want to take that up again?

I have always been into exercise. I've done a lot of strength training, HIIT training, and things like that, and I tried to do something five to six days a week for at least half an hour a day.

However, as I went through my alcohol free journey, I suddenly remembered that I liked running. I haven't run since I was 15 or 16 years old, but I did love it at the time. I loved running. I did cross-country running, 100 meters, 200 meters, and hurdles. I loved running in all its spectrums, but I hadn't done it since I was 16.

So, when I was four months alcohol free, I decided to do a 10k running program. I briefly tried couch to 5k in lockdown before ditching drinking, but I got bored. It wasn't something that I really enjoyed at the time, as there was lots of walking and little running. However, I wanted a new challenge and to rediscover my passion, so this 10k program got me fired up, and at the end of it, I completed my first 10k! I then signed up to do a virtual 10k and received a medal and T-shirt, and I thought, this is amazing.

The next thing I knew, I'd signed up for my first in-person 10k race, which was incredible. The feeling you get when you do a race with like-minded people around you, trying to achieve the same personal goal, is a real joy. I went on to complete my first half marathon and have since gone on to do a few more and have just completed my first marathon! Running has become my passion, and it's something that, as I said, I'd hardly done since I was 16 years old.

The other thing I've really enjoyed doing, which also goes well with running, is yoga. A couple of months into being alcohol free, I discovered online yoga. So, since then, as part of my evening routine, I have practised yoga before bed, and it has become a habit. I've also tried other things, kickboxing, barre, and I continue to do strength training, as exercise is one of the things that I've always loved. Running and yoga are now a huge part of my life.

On the journey, I also started knitting. Again, I hadn't knitted anything for many years, but that's been fun. I've also done a lot of painting.

I've always enjoyed photography, and if you follow me on Instagram (@thrivealcoholfree), you will see my photos. All of the photos on my Instagram page are my photos. I've taken them at some point over the years. So, as you can see, having more than one passion helps you stay inspired, and if for any reason you can't do one of them, you have something else you can turn to that you enjoy doing.

The other thing I've realised when I became alcohol free and is very common for other people who go on this journey, is the personal growth you experience. I've grown so much and wanted to learn and absorb. I've found I'm a lot more curious, and I'm constantly reading. I have read many books, and in the past couple of years, I have read more books in this time than in the past ten years.

Prior to this, I had a lot of "shelf-help" books. I'd buy a lot of books, stick them on my shelf and never read them! However, now it's completely different. I'm just enjoying learning, and reading has inspired me in many ways.

Getting out in nature regularly and walking our dog is also a passion. I walk (well, run) our dog five days a week, but the best part of this is noticing things when I'm out in nature.

If you are thinking about your passion and hobbies, then write down a list of what you enjoy doing. Maybe think about what you liked to do when you were younger and discover new things you may want to try.

Could open-water swimming become your new passion? How about hiking or cycling? Or learning a new skill? Whatever it is, don't be afraid to at least give it a go. You may find you don't like it, or there is something you've never tried that becomes your passion. It's all about experimenting and being alcohol free.

You begin to understand yourself better and maybe find what you thought brought you passion in your authentic self now actually bores you, and something else excites you, and that is ok. It's ok to change. It's ok to become a new person and embody a new identity and find things that empower you in your new identity. You certainly don't have to conform. Go on, discover a new passion today!

Questions to ask yourself:

1. What passion did you have when you were younger that you'd like to try again?
2. What sparks you?
3. What do you think can help you grow on this alcohol free journey?

Action:

- Write a list of 3 things you'd like to try while on this alcohol free journey.

A Cocktail of Clarity Concept

Fun: "Pick a new thing you've been wanting to try for a while and start doing it this weekend." @thrivealcoholfree

> This week has been about trusting the process, being consistent, shifting your mind and aiming for progress, not perfection.
>
> So, what have you been thinking about doing for a while that you keep putting off? Why not start it today? Give it a go and have fun trying something new! Who knows, it may become a new hobby or passion. It could help you grow in some way or start to become the person you aspire to be.

Chapter 10:
1440 Minutes In A Day

"It's worth remembering that it is often the small steps, not the giant leaps, that bring about the most lasting change."

Queen Elizabeth II

One thing I found very early after ditching drinking was that I felt quite bored and realised that I'd been saying I didn't have enough time to do everything for years. Then suddenly, I felt I had a whole lot of time. What's the reason for that, you may be asking yourself? Well, until you take away this one thing from your life, you do not appreciate just how much time you spend, not necessarily drinking but thinking about drinking and not feeling yourself fully because of drinking due to hanxiety, for example, when you suffer from anxiety while feeling hungover the next day and worry about what you said or did.

Drinking takes up way more time than you would ever imagine it does, so you certainly find time on your hands, which you can use to discover passions from Chapter 9, but also you find you want to make the most of your time and use it effectively, not just scroll through social media or buy things online. I'm guilty of this, as I remember in the early days, a large online retailer became a good friend, which we won't name but is also a rainforest. Under the guise of finding alcohol free drinks and exploring new hobbies, I seemed to spend my time (and money) online, which was hardly productive, and I'm sure the number of boxes arriving at our house certainly made my Husband question my spending habits.

Anyway, I digress. With more time on your hands, you can either use them as I've described above or establish a more beneficial routine for all. This is where I recommend creating morning and evening habits that will keep you going as the initial motivation wanes.

So, I thought I'd spend some time in this chapter to discuss how you could establish a routine. However, I want you to be kind to yourself. You will know when the right time is to do this, and you don't need to take on a load of new habits at once. It's all about building a habit, adding to that habit when you're ready and most importantly, once you have established these habits, being consistent, as consistency compounds.

Over the past two and a half years, I have tried various things as part of my morning and evening routine. Some have stuck while others just weren't for me, so I'd suggest being open to trying things and seeing what works best for you and what makes a start and end of your day enjoyable and gives you a sense of calm beyond the madness of the world and everyday life.

Habits have helped me feel grounded. When I started my new job, I was not anxious in any way compared to how I'd felt in my previous company. Setting intentions for a new job that focused on me, such as sticking to healthy habits and continuing to pursue my passions outside of work, enabled me to bring my best self to work.

A couple of principles that I think will be helpful, as a basis for your morning and evening routine, are having time in the morning where you don't wake up with an irritating alarm on your phone which used to immediately give me heart palpitations and then go straight onto the news or social media. This is not, I repeat, not, the most calming way to start your day, and it will instantly put you in a terrible mood. The other thing you may not realise is when you do this. You are also not allowing yourself to take time and think about your thoughts or give yourself a moment to reflect and just breathe before the world's noise infiltrates everything.

This is why thinking about how you spend your first 30 mins to an hour is key to the success of your day. You may think I'm exaggerating, but I kid you not. This is an absolute game-changer. And an easy way to not start the day like that is not to have your phone in the bedroom and keep it in a different room the night before, part of your evening routine. Ok, I hear the protest cries! I couldn't possibly not have my phone with me, by my pillow with all the electric volts pulsing through my head as I sleep, as there could be an emergency. I need my phone to check the time, listen to music before I sleep, and use it as a light to read. Whatever excuse, ask yourself, is it true? Would not having your phone in your room really be such a hardship?

Imagine waking up to a natural light alarm clock where you wake up gently, drink a pint of water (this is great for the brain), spend time breathing, meditating or praying and then pick up your journal and write a gratitude list or you read a chapter of a personal growth paperback for 10 or 20 mins before you do anything else. This allows you to go inwards, think, and maybe even remember what you were dreaming about, which could have some valuable nuggets to help you with your day.

You could then make a coffee, let the light in, give yourself some natural vitamin D, and just take time to notice yourself sipping your coffee while chatting with your Partner. Then potentially you could do some exercise, again as part of your evening routine, you would have put out the clothes and trainers you want to wear to do this, so you're ready to go.

You could just stretch through yoga or do Pilates or a short workout for 10 mins to wake up your body. You don't necessarily need to go for a long run or do a 45-minute intensive workout.

As part of my morning routine, I also now have a cold shower, which is beneficial in so many ways from a health and immune perspective, but don't panic. It's not as horrific as it sounds. I'm sure people have different ways of doing this, but for me, I have a normal shower, and then at the end, I turn it down to cold and stand in it for anywhere between 30 seconds and two mins, depending on my mood or should we say tolerance that day!

Think about how you are nourishing yourself too. I love having a ginger shot in the morning (ginger, lemon and apple) to give me a kick, and at some point in the morning, I like to have green juice if I can.

By creating a routine, you are being intentional about how you want your day to start, giving you a sporting chance of having the day you want. By immediately jumping out of your bed and going on your phone, doom scrolling, sorry to say, but you are not setting yourself up for success, and then you wonder why you are grumpy and find yourself being irritated by the smallest things.

Your evening routine could start with not drinking coffee after 2 pm, as this will help you sleep better. Then you could think about when and what you eat before bed to allow your food to digest. You could say no screen time 30 minutes or an hour before bed and go up to your room, light a candle, listen to a podcast, or read. You could unwind with light yoga or stretching. You could do a breathing exercise or meditate (simply sit still for a couple of minutes and stay present), anything that will help you get into a cosy state and in wind down mode. Then as I mentioned earlier, put your phone in another room and sleep.

I know this may be a lot, and as I said, this does not happen overnight. With habits, you'll find the decisions you make now will determine how you will be in the next ten to twenty years, so you want to be aiming towards the life you want to lead. I certainly don't want you to worry about doing all the things straight away, as I know we all have full lives, so the right time will come, but I wanted to give you some ideas.

We've talked about some of the things I mentioned here in previous chapters, but I wanted to share some breathing exercises with you, as I find these extremely useful. They help reduce stress, tension, overwhelm, and anxiety and keep you calm. Below are three exercises. There are many more out there, so if breathing is something you are interested in learning more about, feel free to explore.

Breathing exercises

- 4-7-8 breathing
    - Breathe in through your nose for a count of four.
    - Hold your breath for seven.
    - Breathe out through your mouth, pursing your lips and making a "whoosh" sound for eight.
    - Repeat three times.

- Box breathing
    - Imagine you are drawing a square (box), and at each corner of the square, follow these steps and go around the edges of the box.
    - Breathe in for a count of four. Hold for four.
    - Breathe out for a count of four. Hold for four.
    - Repeat this as many times as needed, but at least four times, and you will slowly feel calmer.

- Alternate nostril breathing
    - To do this, use your right thumb and ring finger.
    - Cover your right nostril, breathe in, and hold.
    - Switch and cover your left nostril. Pause. Breathe out, then breathe in. Hold.
    - Switch and continue doing this for a few minutes.
    - A way to check you are doing this correctly is anytime you breathe in alternate fingers.
    - Repeat the process for as long as you like but at least for three minutes.

As I mentioned at the start of the chapter, as you suddenly find time on your hands, you could feel bored or look at it differently. You could say to yourself, "There are 1,440 minutes in a day; how am I spending your time?"

I was mulling over this question. We all say we haven't got enough time in the day and can't do certain things, an obvious one that I hear all the time is exercise. But when you think about there being 1,440 mins in a day, 15 to 30 mins of exercise doesn't sound like that much at all. So why does it seem we have no time to look after our health by exercising.

We are all guilty of finding excuses, and the point is we spend the time on what we choose to prioritise, as we all have the same number of hours in a day. So, as you go through this week, maybe think: Am I making the most of my 1,440 minutes in a day?; Am I spending it on what I really want to do?; Will whatever I am spending my time on help move my life in the direction I'm longing for it to go?; Am I using the minutes in a way that helps me to thrive?

Don't worry. I'll be asking myself the same questions too. We all have so much potential inside of us that we are not tapping into. Let's begin to be more intentional about how we spend our time and what we choose to prioritise. You never know how this could help change our world and the world.

Questions to ask yourself:
1. How could having a morning and/or evening routine help you?
2. What one new habit could you introduce in the next week?

3. What would you do and why if you had one extra hour in your day?

Action:

- Incorporate one thing that might be helpful in either the morning or evening to start or add to a routine.

A Cocktail of Clarity Concept

Thought: "Having a morning and/or evening routine allows you to incorporate self-care consistently, and this helps you thrive." @thrivealcoholfree

> Do you have a morning or evening routine? Have you built in habits that help your life versus those that hinder your life?
>
> I found having consistent routines has enabled me to have a fuller life, and it also means that I have activities that I look forward to every day.
>
> It's also something I encourage clients to build in, as it gives them something to focus on in the early days when they find they have more time on their hands or maybe feeling bored, as alcohol is no longer taking up time and space in their minds.
>
> So, if you don't have a routine, start today. Think about one thing you could do in the morning or evening and build on that. Maybe try yoga or meditating, journaling, and writing a gratitude list. These are just some ideas.
>
> When you do these things consistently, life becomes exciting, and you don't want to wake up hungover

or with a foggy head, as you want to do your routine, which is far more fulfilling. Enjoy!

FREEDOM

Find Lasting Joy in All Areas of Life

Chapter 11: Change Your Spots For Good

"One of my favourite things I learnt recently is that the expression 'a leopard doesn't change its spots' is completely false: that a leopard actually does change its spots. I think that's the most beautiful thing. That was something I kind of clung to; the idea that I could make this huge fundamental change in who I was and how I went about life."

Kit Harington

One of the things that kept me drinking, even though I knew I was no longer enjoying it, was the identity I'd created around alcohol.

Everyone expected me to have a G&T or a glass of fizz in hand at social events. I was expected to have a glass of red wine when we were hosting a dinner. It was just who I was and what I did. It made me fun I was the life and soul of the party. It gave me the confidence, I was sophisticated. I could go on and on about all the things I thought alcohol was doing for me and how it was just part of who I was.

So, the thought of changing was never really an option. What would people say, and how would I be without it? You too may be wondering how you'll spend time with your partner, if you'll have anything in common with your friends and telling yourself you like having a glass of wine when you go to your favourite restaurant. But all of this is simply not true, and you can change your identity, like a leopard you can change your spots for good. As the thoughts expressed above are what keeps so many of us stuck.

So, as you've been going through this book, you've picked up tools, tips and resources that you can use to become alcohol free, but there will come a point where you will need to decide and ask yourself, "is it something I carry on with and stay alcohol free and if so, what does that mean in terms of my identity?"

You may have stopped drinking while you've been reading this book, and if you have, I am so excited for you and cheering you on. However, in the not too distant future, you will start to reflect and think, "That was fun for a while, but maybe I will go back to drinking, as surely one won't hurt?" This is known as the fading affect bias, where we start seeing alcohol through rose-tinted glasses, think it wasn't all bad, and remember all the so-called good memories of drinking.

I remember in the first year, many of my friends and family asked, is this it? Will you never drink again? And depending on who asked, I probably gave a different answer, as I wasn't quite ready to commit to forever, and that is perfectly fine. You don't need to. I also want to emphasise that you are probably reading this because you have not hit rock bottom and have chosen to be curious and think about whether alcohol is still serving you. You can, if you would like and want to, have a drink at any point, but I hope I've shown you that you do not need it, and you can and will indeed Thrive Alcohol Free.

Please don't ever look at this as depriving yourself or having to take one day at a time for the rest of your life, as what you will discover is freedom. As you become more aware, have such great clarity and experience amazing things without alcohol, you will eventually get to the point where you realise alcohol is a non-issue. You don't even think about it, and you will see it as a toxic beverage people drink, but as for you, you have chosen a different path and seen the fruits of that, so will not feel the need to go back.

Before you know it, you will have built great memories and associations with being alcohol free, which will enable you to live the life you have always desired, and your new alcohol free identity will be established. You will have changed your spots!

So, if you are just getting started, know that there is a process, but it's worth it and if you have already ditched drinking for a couple of months or so, think about all the benefits you've seen so far and reflect on what would be the reason(s) to go back to it. You will know deep down whether or not your life is physically and emotionally better without alcohol, and hopefully, that will make the decision to stay on this alcohol free path a no-brainer.

All you need is the confidence to start and the courage to continue, and you will soon start to find joy in all areas of your life, which will help you along the way.

I do appreciate that your identity is fairly ingrained, especially if you're in your 30s, 40s and beyond, so you may be thinking this is much easier said than done or thinking you don't even know what your identity is without alcohol, as so many of us have been drinking since our teens, so that is completely understandable.

An exercise that helps my clients is to think about their values. Values are the things that are most important in our lives. The values you have carried through life once you ditch drinking may not be the values you want to carry on with. Your values are key to who you are, how you behave and what you do, and you should be incorporating activities that align with your values every day. This will help you to have a more joyful life, as you live with your full integrity.

As a drinker, the likelihood is there would be times you woke up at 3 am berating yourself, as you had more than the one drink you said you would, or you know the important meeting in the morning will not go as well as you'd like, as you'd promised yourself you would have a clear head, but you actually ended up drinking half a bottle of wine to manage your nerves and anxiety around it.

Without realising, your confidence and trust in yourself diminish over time as you feel you are not doing the things you say you will. However, once you ditch drinking, which is a challenge, you recognise you can do hard things and start to notice you are achieving the commitments you make to yourself and trusting yourself more. This slowly builds your confidence and gives you a new sense of identity.

If we go back to values, it is worth doing an exercise to define and focus on these. I encourage people to take a long list of values and circle 20 that best describe them and that they resonate with. As I mentioned, it may be a shock that these are different from what you think they are when you give yourself time to reflect on them as your identity changes. Once you've selected the 20, go down to ten, then five and rank those five to determine your core values. Finally, think about how you can live out those core values every day in your new alcohol free identity.

In addition to the five, you may also see values in the top ten or twenty that you would never have previously thought were a value. I enjoy taking photos and creating content, and of course, to write a book, you need to be fairly creative! I remember thinking I was not creative and others were creative, but since ditching drinking, creativity is a value of mine and probably has been, but I'd never given myself credit for it.

Values are personal and individual, and there is no right or wrong, but when you are conscious of them, they will help you understand your identity, drive you to make better choices and know what gives you joy and fulfilment, so it is important you are aware of what your values are, as they ultimately, allow you to be and know who you really are.

Below are some example values:

Achievement	Empowerment	Independence	Novelty	Service
Adventure	Enthusiasm	Integrity	Nurturing	Spirituality
Authenticity	Equality	Intuition	Openness	Success
Balance	Faith	Joy	Optimism	Teamwork
Beauty	Freedom	Justice	Order	Tolerance
Bravery	Fun	Kindness	Participation	Trust
Contribution	Generosity	Knowledge	Peace	Uniqueness
Courage	Gratitude	Learning	Perseverance	Unity
Curiosity	Growth	Love	Quiet	Vision
Dedication	Health	Loyalty	Quality	Vulnerability
Dignity	Hope	Meaningful Work	Recognition	Wellbeing
Diversity	Humour	Making a Difference	Respect	Wisdom

If you're wondering how to live out your core values every day to ensure you are honouring them, a practical way of doing this is to add a verb to your core values e.g.

- Live every day with authenticity
- Grow in Faith
- Show generosity
- Find things that bring joy
- Seek opportunities to do meaningful work

I encourage you to really think about and question the values above and what they mean to you and select what you believe now or what you would like to be your top three to five values. Once you have done this, you will be able to prioritise them and build behaviours around your values. This will help you start to embody your new alcohol free identity and ultimately feel comfortable that your spots have well and truly changed, which is something to feel positive and proud about.

Questions to ask yourself:

1. What are three ways you can remind yourself that your identity is now alcohol free?
2. What are your top three to five core values?
3. How can you live those values out every day?

Action

- Write down 20 positive alcohol free memories that you've experienced.

Clarity of Cocktail Concept

Motivation: The pink clouds are worth the wait! @thrivealcoholfree

> People who become alcohol free talk about the pink clouds. This is when you get to a point where you experience euphoria, as the change you've made gives you a sense of happiness and confidence. The

fog has finally lifted, and you feel you can do anything.

The pink clouds may not last forever, but that feeling you get from the realisation of being a new person and having a new identity without the foggy head is amazing.

So, if you are reading this considering becoming alcohol free or have just started on your alcohol free journey, at some point, there will be pink fluffy clouds that you can look forward to, and you will see that being alcohol free is the gift that just keeps on giving!

Chapter 12:
Embrace Your Emotions

"If you aren't in the moment, you are either looking forward to uncertainty or back to pain and regret. I'm very serious about no alcohol. Life is too beautiful."

Jim Carey

For many of us who started drinking in our teens, we have never really learnt to deal with our emotions. It's interesting because they say the brain is not fully formed until you're 25 years old, but if you start drinking, let's say when you officially can (18 years old in the UK and 21 years old in the US), which is rarely the case, our brains are not fully formed, and we are adding poison to our bodies that actually longer-term causes brain shrinkage and all sorts of things that are detrimental to our health.

When you start drinking, the main thing you think it helps with is giving you confidence, helping you to feel less awkward in social settings and reducing anxiety. All of which we now know isn't true, but in theory, if you are now in your 30s, 40s or 50s, the likelihood is alcohol has become a way of numbing emotions and not having to process them, as it's easier to have a glass of wine than sit in your emotions and process them.

So, one of the things I find people struggle with, and I personally felt in the initial days of ditching the booze, is what to do when emotions come over you, and this can involve experiencing several different emotions on the same day.

We need to be comfortable noticing the emotion, sitting in it, letting it wash over us then processing it and finding a way to manage it. Of course, this is easier said than done and no doubt you're reading this and thinking it is just uncomfortable and much easier to have a drink, but this is all part of the alcohol free journey. It helps you to grow as a person and come out the other side much more in tune with yourself, with tools to get you through anything that life throws at you without having to reach for a drink.

If you are in the early days, I suggest you focus on being alcohol free. You will find you may have pangs of regret or shame that come up but don't go deeply into this for now. You can dwell on these at a later point when you are stronger in your alcohol free journey. However, your alcohol free toolkit and HALT will give you ways of dealing with emotions early on. Then you can always think about delving more into these three to six months down the line. At this point, you will feel stronger to explore past emotions, release hurts, forgive people and heal. You can then let go of whatever has happened in the past and focus on the future.

Alcohol is a sedative, and we use it to generally escape reality and numb pain, but we not only numb the negative emotions but also the positive ones, so everything feels a bit flat, a bit meh. As you become stronger in your alcohol free identity, you will become more aware and able to name emotions and learn to manage them better.

As you know, I have seen so many benefits, which have given me so much joy and been so good for my mental and physical wellbeing. Having met several people who have become alcohol free, it seems running, and yoga is something that many people take up once they ditch the booze. They help them manage emotions and mental health, plus give the dopamine hit in a healthier way.

The other thing that is super helpful when it comes to managing emotions is writing down how you're feeling, sitting with them and processing them. So, this is where journalling can be powerful. Ask yourself, "How am I Feeling?" and be honest. I find when I'm asked the question, my instant reaction is "fine, thanks!" However, if you can ask the question, truly consider your response, explore how you are feeling and write it down, this will help you learn to be honest with yourself and find ways to name the emotion and get through it.

So far, a lot of this book has focused on the positives of being alcohol free, which I believe there are many. However, in this chapter, I wanted to take some time to show you that life is not all beer and Skittles, as they say, and life does happen to the best of us, even if we are alcohol free.

When I was approaching 18 months alcohol free, I was diagnosed with a rare illness that was completely unexpected. I had just completed my first half marathon, had been on my first alcohol free abroad holiday, and thoroughly enjoyed it. As far as I was concerned, I was the healthiest I had ever been. I was doing yoga every night, and from a personal growth perspective, I'd just received my certificate for my Alcohol Free Wellbeing Coach training completion and was pretty much on cloud nine.

Well, as you can imagine, when I went to the Doctor the day before my birthday and was told I needed to go to the hospital straight away, this was a bit of a shock. Having done several tests and waited for hours, I was finally diagnosed, and it was the last thing I expected. Over the next few months, there were ups and downs. I had blood taken from me every week and constantly went back and forth to the hospital. I was later diagnosed with something else, so it was a whirlwind of emotions, and I felt out of sorts, not myself.

Being alcohol free, though, was the best thing I could have asked for, as I already had tools that allowed me to cope as best as I could with all the emotions that were running through me. I remember strangers wishing me a happy birthday as the clock turned midnight when I was still in the hospital and feeling like what was happening. I couldn't understand. At the time, breathing techniques, contemplating and praying helped me to believe I would be ok. This was just a blip, but it lasted much longer than expected, and I didn't feel myself for about five months.

Going for walks in nature, reading and doing gentle yoga, once given the go-ahead, helped. I also managed to run a little, which I realised had become so important in my life.

The other thing that helped me is that since I've ditched drinking, I have found that my faith has become a lot stronger, and this has been the main thing that has helped with my emotions, especially as I went through my health issues. The day I was rushed to the hospital was the 10th anniversary of my baptism, as even though I had been brought up in a Christian household, it wasn't until my 30s that I discovered my own faith. So, even though I had no idea what was happening or the diagnosis, I had a strong sense of hope, peace and calm and thought whatever happened, I could trust that I was never alone and it would all work out for good.

This has been my experience of faith, and it brings me a lot of comfort despite what happens on any given day. The first January, after ditching drinking, I read (listened to) the Bible in a month, which set me up for the year. I never would have made the time or thought I had the time to do this. I previously tried to do the bible in one year, which never really happened, so it was wonderful. Since then, I have done it every January to start the year, and I believe it has strengthened my faith and helped me start the year in a way that is positive and helpful for myself.

I fundamentally believe that Jesus loves me. He died for me and rose again, and I believe I have eternal life, which is amazing news! I couldn't write this book without acknowledging this fact, as it wouldn't be authentic, and I know I wouldn't be where I am now without my faith. I certainly wouldn't be able to get through the tough times life has thrown at me without having my faith.

One of the things I've found in many people since they've ditched drinking is that their faith or spirituality has been found or has grown significantly. Suddenly people realise there is a higher power beyond themselves, and they have a purpose that they want and need to live out. It takes you off yourself and makes you look to help and love others. Whatever you believe, I encourage you to develop that more, and if you feel you have no faith or spirituality, you may want to be open and curious to discover what that could mean for you. As you move through your alcohol free journey, you may find this is something you want to explore that grows and will hopefully bring you joy.

Whenever I feel fear, doubt or worry, I find the below declaration helps me to know that I am loved, capable, made for more and can achieve so much more if only I get out of my own way. It is from Lakewood Church:

"I am blessed, prosperous, redeemed, forgiven, healthy, whole, talented, creative, confident, secure, disciplined, focused, prepared, qualified, motivated, valuable, free, determined, equipped, empowered, anointed, accepted and approved. I am not average, not mediocre. I am a child of the most High God. I will become all I was created to be, in Jesus' name!"

I've included this here, as I believe you are ready to hear these affirmations today, and potentially you will keep coming back to them. You are here for such a time as this. Stop holding yourself back, be bold and courageous and do what you know you need to do. You are more than enough, capable and have everything you need inside you.

The combination of being alcohol free and having a strong faith makes me feel like I can deal with anything that comes my way and any emotion I may be feeling on any given day. It's an amazing gift!

During the time of my ill health, something amazing happened. I had been thinking about coaching and how I was going to integrate it more into my day-to-day life, as I really wanted to help people specifically to see the benefits of not drinking, stop holding themselves back and find the courage to live their best life, and that is when I believe the Holy Spirit downloaded to me, what is now, Thrive Alcohol Free. I was flooded with ideas and visions of what this could become and how many people I could help, and this was also probably the start of my thinking about writing this book specifically.

I set up an Instagram account at the time and posted for the first time on my 18-month alcohol free anniversary. I had no idea where it would take me, but I felt this was a way of giving back and sharing what I knew, so I initially started by posting three days a week and then went on to post five days a week, which I have been doing ever since. Seeing these posts, many people would have had no idea there was anything wrong with me. If I'm being honest, it also took my mind off myself and what was happening to me at the time.

Later in the year, I bought a few web domains and created my Thrive Alcohol Free website. I started to coach people specifically in this space. This episode, although at the time, was painful, emotional and unexpected but could have been a lot worse, helped me to reset and think about what was important. It made me consider where I wanted to leave a legacy and how I genuinely could help people. So, as they say, things tend to happen for you and not to you, and if you go with that thought, you never know what will come out the other side. The likelihood is it will be better in some way than before. I had a choice to either wallow in my sorrows and have a pity party or do something positive with them, and I chose to believe bigger and think about something beyond me.

We all have options on how we react to things that happen, especially when they are unexpected, such as illness, grief and loss of a job or relationship. However, being alcohol free helps you process things in a much more positive way. It gives you the tools to understand how you feel, manage those feelings and not turn to alcohol to numb out the pain.

There are 35 different types of emotions, with the eight primary ones being joy, trust, fear, surprise, sadness, disgust, anticipation and anger. Joy is the opposite of sadness. Fear is the opposite of anger. Anticipation is the opposite of surprise, and disgust is the opposite of trust (Plutchik's Wheel of Emotions).

Delving into emotions and being able to name them does help us clarify how we feel and not assume how we are feeling. However, we tend to go to "I'm happy" or "I'm sad" again because we never really learnt the tools to name and process emotions and automatically thought having a drink would numb them, so we don't have to deal with the emotion. Are you feeling fear, dread, anger, anxiety, inadequacy, frustration, or tearfulness? What is the reason? Can you delve deeper, write it down and think about what would help to move the emotion to where you'd prefer to be?

Many people are frightened of emotions and think that if they are not always happy, there is something wrong with them. However, we were made to have emotions, and that is one of the joys of being human. There is no such thing as a bad or wrong emotion. It's what we do with them that matters. Emotion, not logic, inspires action.

The worst thing you can do is ignore the emotion and let it fester, as you could end up getting to the point you want to numb it and then find you just reach for a glass, as this is a quick fix.

Another tool that is helpful for managing emotions is the Emotional Freedom Technique (EFT). It helps to reduce anxiety. It is effectively tapping, and you use tapping points to feel calmer. Start by tapping the side of your hand in a karate chop and say the mantra: *"In this moment, even though I am feeling X, I deeply and completely love and accept myself"*. Repeat this three times. This is the setup.

Then tap on the crown of your head, saying the same words three times; then tap the side of your eyebrows where it meets the nose again repeating the mantra; then tap the side of your eye saying the words; then tap under the eye with the mantra; tap under the nose saying the words, then tap under the lips on the chin repeating the mantra; tap on the collar bone saying the words; tap under the arm with the mantra; and then take a deep breath and repeat the mantra. You can repeat the words again and finally end with: *"I want to focus on gratitude, I want to shine my light."*

Being more present has allowed me to notice and feel all my emotions. I have become comfortable sitting with my emotions and processing them. It's strange at first because we are so used to numbing our emotions. As a society, we drink alcohol to celebrate, commiserate, and grieve and never give ourselves the time to process our emotions and thoughts. Being alcohol free helps you to sit with and process your emotions. It also helps you be more in the moment, notice how you feel and the things around you. For me, being present in the day is the most important thing.

Questions to ask yourself:

1. How do you want to feel on a daily basis on your alcohol free journey?
2. What emotions do you want to have?
3. Is there anything you can do now to generate this?

Action

- Think about the emotions that are coming up for you this week. Consciously think about how you react to them and manage them.

Clarity of Cocktail Concept

Thought: Being alcohol free enables us to live joyfully, which in turn improves our mental and physical wellbeing. @thrivealcoholfree

> How are you feeling today? Have you been feeling stressed, overwhelmed and anxious? Did you know you have the power to choose joy?
>
> Choosing to make time each day for small moments of joy can help you cope with the challenges you face and keep you resilient.
>
> If you can intentionally do this and create rituals that work for you, this will help you maintain a joyful day and manage your negative emotions. Alcohol is a depressant and can exacerbate anxiety and depression, so by letting alcohol go, it helps you to naturally find joy and live a happier life where you thrive.

Chapter 13:
The Future Is Bright

"There are far better things ahead than we ever leave behind."

C.S. Lewis

Before ditching drinking, you may have found that you feared trying new things or thought you were afraid of certain things. However, when you become alcohol free, you realise how much you have achieved and can celebrate how far you've come. As alcohol is so embedded in our society, doing this one thing is quite a big ask and can be quite challenging, but as they say, we can do hard things. Therefore, many people start to think, if I can do this, what else could I do that I didn't think possible? This is where the magic happens!

You are more than capable and courageous enough to do anything you want to do. Once you start to feel comfortable being alcohol free, you begin to think and ask yourself, what else can I do and achieve? How could I reach those goals that I've been thinking about, and you realise the future is indeed bright?

But where do I start? If, like me, you were just going through the motions and not being intentional about what you really wanted for many years, it can be difficult to know what goals you want to set yourself or what you would like to accomplish.

Once you've been alcohol free for a while, you'll find, at some point, real clarity, focus, and awareness become the norm, and you will start to ponder on those life questions. I would suggest you consider where you see your alcohol free journey going and how long you want to commit to being alcohol free.

As you go along the journey, make it a priority to commit to the next milestone you want to achieve. If you have ditched drinking for 30 days, why not commit to 60 or 90 days? Next, if you've reached 60 days, commit to being alcohol free until at least 100 days. It's important you are conscious of this commitment, which doesn't necessarily mean needing to track and tick off every day, but it does help you focus and be mindful of fading affect bias. You don't want to start to see things with rose-tinted glasses, think you've been alcohol free long enough and decide to have a drink having seen some of the benefits. It's all too easy to start to think it wasn't that bad. It didn't really hold me back. It was fun. Moderation will be fine. However, I have seen people do this and very quickly slip back to old habits of drinking way more than they'd like to and come back realising that they weren't missing out after all.

As I've said, you can absolutely have a drink tonight to see how you feel, but what would be the reason to, now you know what you know? It is a choice, but all I would say is before you reach for a glass or think it was the best thing ever, question what you really want or what feeling you are trying to create and first go to the tools and tips you've read in this book before going down that route. Also, play it forward to the next day and three or six months down the line. Is it worth it?

If you're thinking, what do I want to focus on, or what are your goals? As I mentioned, when asked, many people realise they haven't thought about it for a while or don't know. So, one of the things I encourage my clients to do is complete a Wheel of Life. This is for them to reflect on where they are in life and shows them that life isn't just made up of one or two things like career and family. Unless we look at all elements of our life and find balance across all these things, we will never live the full life we deserve.

So, what is the Wheel of Life? The Wheel of Life is a framework where we look at the eight most important areas in our life, which we can select and use to determine where we are now and where we want to be. This helps us to be clear on our current situation and see how far off we are from our ideal future selves. Below I suggest areas you could focus on but feel free to think about what you want to prioritise in your life:

- Family
- Health
- Faith / Spirituality
- Career / Business
- Self-Care
- Personal Growth
- Finances
- Friends / Socialising

Once you've decided on your categories, create a circle and split it into eight parts and assign each part of the circle with a category you have selected, then inside the circle, add one to ten, with one being, this is not where you want it to be at all versus ten, which means you are exactly where you want to be in this area of your life.

Reflect on where you think your life is in each category, and mark where you believe you are right now. Then think about where you want them to be and add another mark, potentially in a different colour of your ideal state, in a timeframe that suits you, e.g. 90 days from now. You will then clearly see where the gaps are and be able to think about how to close those gaps. This will give you the areas you want to prioritise and potentially the goals you then want to set.

Don't overwhelm yourself, so select one to three areas you want to focus on and how you can do a small thing to start moving towards your ideal number and go from there.

My clients find this to be a useful tool to use and see it as a place to start once they have the head space and clarity to think about what is next. It also becomes clear that there is no balance, and they are potentially striving or putting all their attention in one or two areas and finding they are burnt out and exhausted. Balance in life is so important and makes such a difference. I do hope this is helpful to you.

The future is bright, and you have so much to look forward to and accomplish now that alcohol is becoming less important in your life, and a world you have not seen for a while where you can go after your dreams again is right in front of you.

Questions to ask yourself:
1. How are you feeling about being alcohol free? What has changed?
2. Where do you see your alcohol free journey going, and at this moment in time, how long do you want to commit to being alcohol free for?

3. What can you do if you start to experience fading affect bias?

Action

- Complete the Wheel of Life based on areas of your life that are most important to you and plot where you are today and where you would like to be in a timeframe in the future. Think about where you'd like to focus your attention and how you can start to work towards reaching your ideal state for each area.
- Below is a template you can use:

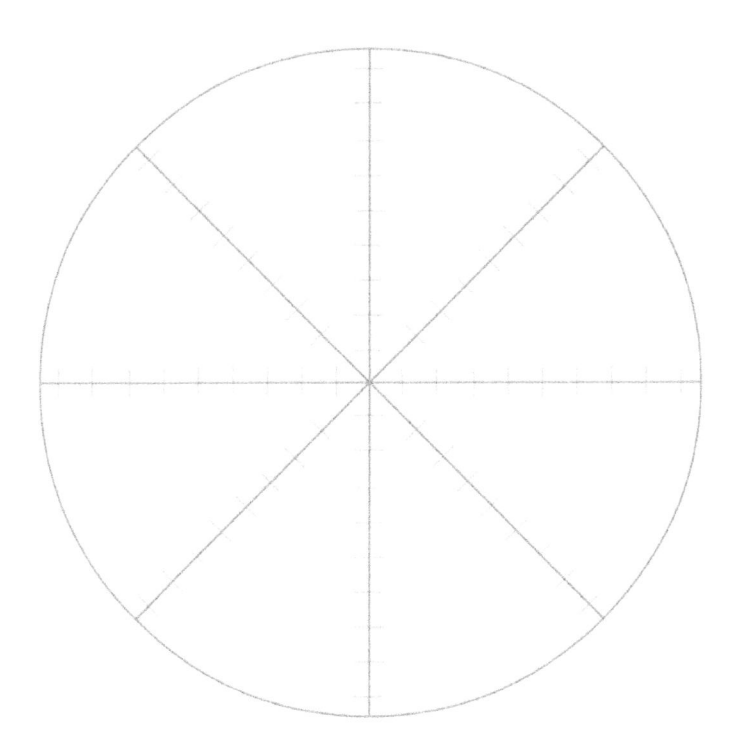

Clarity of Cocktail Concept

Motivation: Imagine life without alcohol, dare to dream what's your life will look like and visualise how you'll feel. Life is meant to be amazing, and you can design it. @thrivealcoholfree

> Anyone who has been on this journey and stayed alcohol free will agree that making this choice is life changing, and their whole perspective shifts. We start to realise that we are in control of our destiny and life can be anything we want.
>
> We realise, when pondering if we can do or try something new or go after a dream, that we actually can! So, if you have ditched drinking while reading this book, a huge congratulations for taking this step. I'm so excited for you! Please keep going. Dare to dream; no doubt you will experience an incredible shift and not look back!

Chapter 14:
Dream Big

"Where there is no vision, the people perish."

King Solomon (Proverbs 29:18)

I discovered vision boards during the first December that I was alcohol free, a month or so after I ditched drinking. This was a completely new experience for me, and I realised I had been coasting along in life, not really being intentional about designing my life and not knowing what I really wanted my life to look like. My focus had been my career when it came to setting goals, but life is so much more than that.

It's so easy to just drift from one month to the next, one year to the next and not have a clear vision of where you're going and before you know it, you're 80 years old full of regrets about not going after what you really wanted or realise that you've been living someone else's dreams or living up to society's expectations never having expressed who you really are or truly discovered what you actually wanted. Life is short, and it's easy to find ourselves never stopping, coming up for air and taking time to reflect and discern where we want to go, so I urge you, please don't let this be you.

You are here for a reason and a purpose. You have gifts only you can share with the world, and you deserve to live the fullest, most amazing life beyond what you could imagine.

Being alcohol free can help expand your vision, live your best life and reach your full potential.

I've found that around ten weeks of not drinking alcohol, people start to think about their purpose and what they want to achieve. This is because you have greater clarity and awareness and more time to think about what you want to do. In addition to that, your vision expands, as you realise if you can do this, you allow yourself to believe you can do anything. Being alcohol free is a superpower!

You may be asking yourself, what is a vision board? There are many ways to do it, but I thought it was best to talk through how I do it to give you something practical to take away. So, I created my vision board for 2021, and everything changed.

I bought a corkboard, and I added the year. I thought about it and came up with my word for the year, which in 2021, mine was "Transform" and wrote a short paragraph on "My hope for 2021 is…". I then created categories of my life to focus on. I selected: Family, Faith, Health, Self-Care, Career, Finance and Personal Growth. For each area, I added pictures, inspiring words, and Bible verses and then at the bottom of the board, I put down the top three overall goals that I wanted to achieve.

As the year went on, things started to happen. For example, I had put a picture of someone taking a leap over water from one side to another, and that exact picture was on a programme that I watched on the impact of Coaching. As one of the goals in this Personal Growth category, I had written, "To become a Life Coach, so I can help others, " but I had no idea how that would happen and where I would find the time and space to do that while working full time. However, long story short, the opportunity presented itself for me to start a course at the end of January, I found a way to make it work, and I went on to become an accredited Transformational Coach! It may sound woo-woo or unbelievable, but the majority of the things on that vision board had come to fruition by the end of the year. This was amazing to me, but it does go to show that so many of us are not reaching our full potential because our vision is limited.

As I was writing this book, I went back to my 2021 vision board and realised that under "Health", the three goals I'd written were:

- To run the London Marathon
- To exercise 6 days a week
- To practice Pilates and Yoga

Reading these back now, it's very strange as the only thing I was doing at that point in time was exercising six days a week and dabbling in Pilates. I had not started running or doing yoga yet for some reason, I'd written these.

I started to do yoga in January 2021 and then began running in February 2021. There was no way I was ready to take on a marathon, but it was on my vision board. However, by taking the first step of saying what you'd like to happen, even if it does sound impossible, it puts something in your subconscious, which makes you want to act on it.

By beginning these two things, I had no idea where they would lead. I didn't do a marathon in 2021, but I did complete a few 10Ks, which were achievements on their own. However, later that year, I got a ballot place for the London Landmarks Half Marathon in April 2022. This was after entering because a friend said I should try, not really knowing anything about it! Ironically, I got a place, but my friend didn't!

So, I trained for the Half Marathon and finished that in 2:06:51, which I was amazed at. It was such a great atmosphere, and wonderful to see the city I've worked in for 20 years in a different light. I went past places I'd worked, visited and eaten in, bringing back many memories.

I then went on to do the Oxford Half Marathon in October 2022, which was slightly slower in 2:26:19 but considering the six months I'd had from a health perspective and having not really trained anywhere near as much as the previous Half, I was extremely proud of myself and again, amazing to see this city from a different perspective.

I had entered the London Marathon ballot at the beginning of October thinking, wouldn't it be great to do having done two half marathons this year? I thought at least I had some experience now of running, but I knew a marathon was another level, a completely different ball game, and I wondered if I was actually ready for that.

However, I knew the chances of getting a ballot slot were fairly slim but applied after thinking you needed to be in it to win it, and about a week after doing the Oxford Half, I found out I'd got in!!! I was going to do the London Marathon in April 2023! What?!!!

The cynic in you may say the vision board didn't work because it was on your 2021 board, and this wasn't until 2023, but it goes to show, that things tend to happen when you are ready and prepared for them and not necessarily in our own timing. I probably would have struggled to do a marathon in 2021, as I hadn't even started running, in hindsight, it was a bit of a pipe dream but it set the wheels in motion.

So, if you would indulge me here, I want to tell you a bit about the experience of running a marathon, as I think it shows the commitment, focus, clarity and awareness that you get from being alcohol free and helps you to achieve anything. A friend of mine told me after I'd finished that only 0.2% of the world's population has completed a marathon, which I thought was unbelievable! Hopefully, this inspires you.

As I've described, my marathon journey started way before I even got a ballot slot. I had been running regularly for a year and a half or so, which had become a great way to relax. It made me feel good, gave me time to think and just started to become a habit, which I missed if I didn't do it, but the real training started 18 weeks before the big day.

I had committed to doing a marathon training plan, which was five days of running a week, including three recovery runs, a one-speed run and a long run. At the start, I thought I'd do something similar to the London Landmarks Half Marathon training: I'd do five days a week for the first month and then go down to three days.

However, as the weeks went on, I committed to doing all five runs each week and stuck to this, which looking back, I'm not sure how I managed it. I started training in mid-December, so as you can imagine, I ran in the snow, rain, wind and all other weather in between. I ran when I was feeling under the weather. I even ran on a treadmill for a few times when I was travelling for work, which I never did, just to ensure I got my five runs in that week. Having flown back, I then did a 75-minute run and a 30k run that weekend!

I've always been determined and would probably be described as a Type A personality and have achieved quite a lot in my life, so this is a trait of mine. However, since becoming alcohol free, I have found it's so much easier to commit and dedicate myself to something and really go after it.

Over the course of the plan, I completed 90 runs, including the London Marathon and covered a distance of 738k!!! When I see this written down on paper, that is a lot of runs, but with anything, I just took each day at a time and trusted the process. The first run was 10 mins, and it built up from there, so being present in the moment and focusing on what I needed to do now, as opposed to thinking about running a marathon in 18 weeks was helpful.

By the end, the longest runs I had completed were two 30k and one 32k runs. Although, one of those weeks, I only needed to do a 26.2k run instead of a 30k run, but a friend of mine who is a marathon and Iron Man finisher encouraged me to do 30k, so I did!

All in all, I learned a lot about myself through this experience. I am so grateful, as it helped me appreciate my body and health. I realised I could run quite happily in the rain, and in a strange way, it was quite enjoyable. I learnt about fuelling properly with gels and chews, plus using electrolytes effectively to replenish the salt you lose from sweating, and then the big day arrived.

There was a lot of hanging around, and my Husband and Daughter escorted me to the start, which was much appreciated. I was feeling nervous but excited. After all the work, I knew I was ready and thought I'd be able to do it, but the unknown, having never done a marathon before, made me wonder if I truly could.

As we were waiting for me to eventually head to my wave, it started to rain, but it was fairly light, so I thought it would stop. Anyway, I said goodbye to my family, headed to the wave, then the heavens opened, and it poured. To say we were drenched in heavy rain before we even started was an understatement, but as I mentioned earlier, I'd trained in the rain, which was a blessing, so it didn't bother me, although I hoped it would stop soon.

I crossed the starting line and was off! It didn't really sink in that I was running the London Marathon. It felt very surreal. As I ran, the rain kept coming, and there was no let up, but what amazed me was the number of people that came out to support us despite the weather. It was astonishing.

At around 10k, I got to Cutty Sark, and this was the first place where the crowds and sounds were epic, but as I turned right and saw Tower Bridge in front of me, I remember just saying, "Wow!" to myself. To run across Tower Bridge with all the crowds cheering us on was just amazing and once you crossed the bridge you reached the halfway mark, but there was a lot to go.

As the miles went on, my legs started to feel heavy, but I was determined to keep running, and so I did. The rain subsided a little but then came down again at Canary Wharf. Knowing I was three quarters of the way through, I just kept going. I tried to keep up with my carb, sodium and fluid intake, but at one point felt a bit like I'd had too much, so I backed off and just kept running. I backed off when I needed to, then picked it up again, tried to focus ahead, and just breathed while trying to use my arms as efficiently as possible to help me run. These were all things I'd learnt during my training.

When I had about 2k to go, my legs felt extremely heavy, but when I saw the Houses of Parliament ahead, I knew I was nearly done. I have to say, seeing 600m to go, then getting to Buckingham Palace and turning right seeing 395 yards to go and the finish line, was the most epic and relieving feeling! Crossing that line was an incredible feeling and completely surreal. Having the medal placed around my neck was fantastic, and I felt incredibly proud of myself. I finished the London Marathon, which people say is the best in the world and my first marathon, in 4:34:17, which wasn't too shabby! Later I would find out that this was also the largest Marathon in terms of the number of runners (48,000) since it started in 1981. I was also part of history!

So, if you have a dream, maybe it's running a marathon or something else, no matter how big or impossible it may seem, I'd say write it somewhere and go after it. Even though the first step may seem too small or you don't know when you will achieve the dream, I promise you, it will happen at some point.

I heard it said that your inner vision sets the limit on your life, so I would encourage you to expand your vision and create a vision board to see what happens.

With my coaching clients, I work through a visualisation exercise, where they picture themselves at a point in the future, maybe six months ahead, and I get them to think about where they are, how it feels and what they are thinking about at that moment. I then ask them to go backwards, a month at a time and think about the key thing they are doing, how they feel, where they are and what they are thinking and work backwards. This then leads them back to the present day, where they describe how they feel now, and it tends to enable them to feel confident, trust the process towards the outcome they are looking for and believe they will achieve what they plan to. They are now fully committed.

Visualisation meditations help you imagine yourself in a place and get you to think about your future self. I also find writing letters to your future self to be an encouraging activity, that helps you focus on what you want to achieve. I do this at the end of every year and read it the following year, which inspires me. Finally, writing your goals as if you have already achieved them is a way to get your brain to think in the way you want, so things start to happen. These all help you gain clarity, focus and be intentional. When you visualise, you materialise!

It's easy to think something good will happen eventually, and that may be the case, but why are we not more intentional about making our lives better? Having goals and then making small incremental changes can make such a difference in our lives, and you can look back a year or two later and be amazed by the changes that have happened.

You can choose to fully live the life you really want. So, what is your big dream? It's time to go after it.

Having read this book, I hope and pray that you are inspired, have found it useful, and it's given you a different perspective of what being alcohol free really means. Doing this one thing leads to so much more. Making this decision is just the start, and the real beauty is what comes next.

You have a wonderful opportunity to go against the grain and do something different. You do not need to follow the crowd. You can take your own path, even if it feels uncomfortable. If everyone around you drinks, you will be doing something that can feel completely alien after so many years. But trust me. It is so worth it. You are worth it. The amazing life that is waiting for you on the other side is one hundred per cent worth it.

If you take this step, I know you will not regret it, and life will never be the same. You were not born to be average or mediocre. You can achieve great things. Go on, be different from the crowd. Why fit in when you were born to stand out!

I look forward to hearing your stories as you go on this exciting alcohol free journey. You can ditch drinking for good, embody your new alcohol free identity and find lasting joy in all areas of your life. Be brave and take the first step. I'm rooting for you and cheering you on!

Questions to ask yourself:

1. What is your vision for the next year and which areas do you want to set goals against?
2. What is your big dream?
3. What one small change or step can you take today?

Action

- Now create a vision board for the next year with pictures and quotes for the areas of your life that resonate and your top three overall goals. Visualise where you want to be six months, one year, two years and five years down the line. N.B. people overestimate what they can do in a year and underestimate what they can do in five, so think about this carefully and consider how being alcohol free could help you get there and thrive.

Clarity of Cocktail Concept

Motivation: Is there something you think is impossible but would like to do? Why not think about how you could achieve it? @thrivealcoholfree

>We all have dreams but think that some are impossible and we could never achieve them. However, what if you woke up and thought maybe it isn't impossible and could actually go after it?
>
>I heard someone say only the impossible is worth doing. One area that improves when you are alcohol free is your REM sleep, which helps deep sleep and is when you dream. So, by ditching alcohol, you literally start to dream again!
>
>The difference is you are also suddenly brave and feel you have a superpower, so you take the first step towards what once seemed impossible and would never have allowed yourself to dream in a past life.
>
>You can do anything, and all dreams are possible. So, what is your impossible dream? Go do the impossible!

Closing Thoughts: (Alcohol Free) Gin Clear!

"Step out of the history that is holding you back. Step into the new story you are willing to create."

Oprah Winfrey

I hope A Cocktail of Clarity has shown you how to Thrive Alcohol Free and inspired you to at least explore what being alcohol free could do for your life. As a cocktail contains many ingredients, you've seen that to gain real clarity from being alcohol free, it isn't just one thing but many things that lead to this. Creating a new identity and embodying that identity, building new habits in your life, discovering passions, changing your limiting beliefs around alcohol, determining your values and envisioning a life that is fully lived without it.

Becoming alcohol free could be the absolute best thing you will ever do. It is life-changing, and you will realise it is also your superpower. Ditching drinking may feel like an impossible task, but hopefully, having read this book, you can take steps to get through that initial period because this is just the start.

It will feel uncomfortable at first, you may still have cravings, and you might not sleep well for a couple of months, but once you are through that and come out the other side, it will be time to live your life, a full life that is vibrant and you can design it in any way you like. Once this happens, there is no doubt you will Thrive, reach your full potential and live your best life alcohol free! You will find you are a different person, but all you have done is find your authentic self, the true unique you who has always been inside but is finally here for such a time as this.

If you have been thinking about how your drinking is making you feel or questioning whether alcohol is still serving you, I would encourage you to ditch the booze for a defined period (60 or 100 days, maybe), make it a non-negotiable and see how you feel.

From a personal perspective, there are so many benefits that I've seen, as I've gone from 21 days to 30 days, to 60 days, to 90 days, to 6 months, then a year, and now two and a half years. I can genuinely say I'm a different person. I am so grateful for the changes and the opportunities becoming alcohol free has brought, and don't tell anyone, but I hear it keeps getting better!

So, I want to leave you with this final action: sit, reflect and imagine what could happen if you had full clarity in your life. Could you Thrive?

A Cocktail of Clarity Concept

Question: "Imagine what could happen if you had clarity in your life. Could you Thrive?" @thrivealcoholfree

> At 100 days alcohol free, I wrote: *"I feel like there's a clarity I haven't had in years, and I feel less anxious but just generally feel there is so much more I can do, and I'm excited about what's to come!"*
>
> When I hit 200 days alcohol free, I wrote this: *"Although it's been hard at times and I'm still a little nervous about going back into the "new normal", on*

the whole, knowing that others who have gone before me all have such positive stories have kept me going, and the changes and mental clarity that I've experienced have been amazing. It's so worth it!"

What would it be like if you were to get clarity on what you really want in life? Would this help you grow in the clarity of who you are?

Clarity is everything! I truly believe being alcohol free brings real clarity, and your eyes are wide open to endless possibilities. It's an incredible feeling.

About The Author

Dupe Witherick is an accredited Alcohol Free Wellbeing and Transformational Coach and Founder of Thrive Alcohol Free Ltd. She is married, a Mum to a nine-year-old daughter and has a black Labrador. She lives in Oxfordshire, UK and is an avid runner and yogi. She has a strong faith and believes she would not be where she is today without the help of the Holy Spirit.

Since becoming alcohol free in 2020, she has seen for herself the many benefits this brings. Dupe is now on a mission to help others who may be questioning their relationship with alcohol, wondering if it is still serving them and thinking there is more to life. Her mission is to help as many people as possible Thrive, reach their full potential and live their best life alcohol free.

She does this through her One-to-One and Group Coaching Programs and gets the message out through social media and podcasts. In her coaching, she helps high-achieving women who are questioning their relationship with alcohol, feeling stressed and overwhelmed with life, wondering if there is more to life than where they are now, to discover that by ditching this one thing, everything changes for the better. It is the catalyst for them to move towards the life that, deep down, they have been desiring for a while but have felt stuck or held back from going after. Inside the programs, she walks through her signature THRIVE AF method, so you can finally ditch drinking and begin to Thrive Alcohol Free.

Other Services By The Author

Dupe Witherick helps high-achieving, empathic professional and entrepreneurial women who are feeling stuck, not progressing as quickly as they'd like in their career or business and potentially experiencing imposter syndrome or anxiety to go from surviving and juggling work and life to constantly thriving.

If you know you want to stop drinking alcohol and you'd like to learn alternatives to drinking, these programs will help you thrive, reach your full potential and live your best life alcohol free.

Go from using alcohol as a crutch to ditching drinking for good, embodying a new alcohol identity and finding lasting joy in all areas of life to Thrive Alcohol Free. All while managing your emotions, discovering new passions and building new habits moving towards the life you were born to live.

Dupe does this through her Alcohol Free Wellbeing and Transformational Coaching and offers the following:

- One-Off One-to-One Intensive Clarity Session
- One-to-One Coaching Program
- Thrive Alcohol Free Society – Signature Premium Group Program

Transformational Coaching explores a client's inner world of beliefs, assumptions, values and expectations to create greater life possibilities.

If you make a commitment to being alcohol free for a period of time and potentially beyond, you don't need to do it alone, and the above can help you.

Dupe is also a Guest Speaker on Podcasts, has appeared on TV and has been featured in magazines.

As a bonus and thank you for reading this book, head over to:
https://www.thrivealcoholfree.com/acocktailofclaritybook
and claim your free resources to help you continue on your journey.

Becoming alcohol free is the catalyst to everything else that will help you thrive in all aspects of life. So, if you'd like to find out more about how to do this, and connect / work with Dupe, use the following channels:

- Website: www.thrivealcoholfree.com
- Email: dw@thrivealcoholfree.com
- Instagram: @thrivealcoholfree

One More Thing Before You Go...

If you enjoyed reading this book or found it useful, we'd be very grateful if you'd post a short review on Amazon.

Your support really does make a difference, and we read all the reviews personally. Reviews will also help "A Cocktail of Clarity" get into the hands of those who need it.

If you'd like to leave a review, then all you need to do is click the review link on Amazon here:

https://amzn.to/3VbjqmD

Thanks again for your support!

Now go, Thrive, reach your full potential and live your best life Alcohol Free! You have no idea how happy it will make you and me! Let me know if this book helped you get started and keep going.

Scan the code to get your thank you message from the author.

Printed in Great Britain
by Amazon